Al Biruni   Karl Marx

Sir William Jones

Julius Wellhausen   Rudolf Otto   Immanuel Kant   Rudolf Bultmann   Emile Durkheim   EB Tylor

Embarking Upon the
Study of Religion

Nietzsche

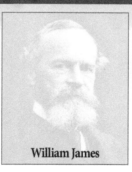
William James

by Tim J. Davis

Elizabeth Cady Stanton   Sir James Frazer

Matilda Joslyn Gage   Kierkegaard

Max Weber

Leopold von Ranke   Hannah Adams

Max Muller   David Hume

Copyright © 2017 by Tim J. Davis

Sentia Publishing Company has the exclusive rights to reproduce this work, to prepare derivative works from this work, to publicly distribute this work, to publicly perform this work, and to publicly display this work.

All rights reserved. No part of this publication may be reproduced, stored in a retrieval system, or transmitted, in any form or by any means, electronic, mechanical, photocopying, recording, or otherwise, without the prior written permission of the copyright owner.

Printed in the United States of America

ISBN 978-0-9977857-5-3

Contents

1. Religious Traditions of Others....................pg. 1

2. Refining Academic Approaches................pg. 21

3. Defining Religion..................................pg. 57

4. What are the Differences Between
   Philosophy, Theology, and Religion?............pg. 69

5. From Phenomenology to the Void.............pg. 89

6. Questions and Perspectives for
   Contemporary Religion.........................pg. 115

7. Methodology and Objectivity in
   The Study of Religion..........................pg. 145

1

The Religious Traditions of Others
Before *The Study of Religion* Became an Academic Discipline

The academic study of *world religions* or *comparative religion* is a fairly new field of inquiry. It attempts to analyze religious practices from a variety of perspectives, viewpoints and disciplines, sometimes looking for common elements in the human experience. Academic departments at most European universities only began to include courses in the comparative *study of religion* in their curriculums during the second half of the 19th century. Up until that time there were all kinds of religious studies, but people focused mainly on investigating aspects of their own traditions and worldviews. Philosophy and theology, around since the ancient and medieval worlds, have greatly informed modern religious scholarship. In fact, critical methods of analysis used in religious investigations today would not have been possible without these early areas of inquiry. Other academic fields like anthropology, art history, sociology, psychology, along with the historical-critical method for interpretation of the Judeo-Christian scriptures, all made their debut in higher education during the 1800's. Scholars in these fields also worked to investigate aspects of religion that pertained to their own disciplines. In fact, much of the early groundbreaking work in the *study of religion* came from early anthropologists, sociologists and psychologists.

From the outset we need to understand that the major influences upon academic religious study (actually up until almost the 1970's) came from white Christian men who were products of European educational systems. This factor clearly shapes the evolution of the discipline. Prior to the 1800's, there is a rather extensive backdrop that needs to be unfolded in order to understanding how the *study of religion* came to be a science and an academic discipline. We will focus on that history in our first two chapters. Going as far back as the ancient world, accounts of interactions with the religions of others have been well documented. Reasons for intentional interest in the religions of other cultures range from the necessity of understanding others in order to allow for interaction and exchange, to issues of tolerance and maintaining peace in the building of empires, contact for the purposes of conquest and conversion, affirming one's own religious truth while condemning the practices of others as false, simple curiosity, and also in a more idealized quest for a realization of religious harmony.

Tolerance and Peace in the Process of Empire-Building

Humans have had been intensely writing about religion and producing sacred texts for some 3,5000 years, but there was rarely much comparative study done outside of one's own religion (unless one converted to another ideology). Obviously, there were some exceptions. For example, the ancient Romans engaged in attempts to understand the numerous religious practices of their empire. This was done primarily in order to keep peace and accommodate the various beliefs of their citizenry. The orator and writer Cicero (106-43 BCE) called this fellow Romans *religiossima gens* (the most religious people). Cults to the Egyptian goddess Isis, Anatolian Cybele, the Persian god Mithra, and Greek god Dionysius appeared throughout Italy. While they were not in fact charitable toward all cults and beliefs (particularly the new ones like Christianity), the Romans did work to accept and embrace multiple religious systems and philosophies within their empire without much critical concern. Likewise, for the sake of unity and facility of expansion, some 500 years earlier, the Persians (550-330 BCE) had shown a similar openness and tolerance for the sake of empire-building. The best examples in Persia might be the growth of the dualistic religion of Zoroastrianism, allowing the Hebrews to return to a practice of their faith, and the restoration of their holy temple in the city of Jerusalem following the Babylonian Captivity (598-538 BCE).

Throughout much of the medieval period, Islam showed great tolerance for Judaism and Christianity. This was likely because they believed they worshipped the same God. The phrase *People of the Book* used in the Quran (compiled from oral and written sources between 610 and 644) and the Hadith (which began to be orally compiled as early as 632) refers to those people using monotheistic scriptures (Jews, Christians and Arabic Sabians) that share connections with the Muslim tradition. Medieval Islam is for the most part noted for this spirit of acceptance of people from other monotheistic traditions within its empires and caliphates. Some of this tolerance was extended to Zoroastrianism as well.

Interest in the Religion of Others

Tolerance, refutation, and general interest are quite different motivations. As early as the 11th century, the Persian Muslim scholar Al-Biruni (973-1048) was doing detailed comparative anthropological work on religions and cultures of the Middle East and Indian subcontinent (Hinduism, Buddhism, Zoroastrianism and Islam). It seems he was driven mainly by interest, believing that there was something common that tied peoples and cultures together. A polymath, he composed over 100 works on diverse topics from history to science, medicine, mineralogy, astrology, math calendars, and geography. Al-Biruni traveled through India making notes of the culture, collecting books and studying Sanskrit. He also translated Hindu works into Arabic. His work on India includes an encyclopedic collection *Tatikh Al-Hindi* (History of India) in which he deals with historical, cultural and religious topics. It's longer name *Taqīq mā li-l-hind min maqūlah maqbūlah fī al-'aql aw mardhūlah* translates as "Verifying All That the Indians Recount, the Reasonable and the Unreasonable". The title is most often simply abbreviated to Al-Hindi, or in English, *The India*. In his introduction to the work he states his desire to report objectively:

> This book is not a polemical one. I shall not produce the arguments of our antagonists in order to refute such of them as I believe to be in the wrong. My book is nothing but a simple historic record of facts. I shall place before the reader the theories of the Hindus exactly as they are and I shall mention in connection with them similar theories of the Greeks in order to show the relationship existing between them.[1]

Interestingly he treats the religion of India as a single tradition. Muslim scholars before him had attempted to divide their descriptions in to as many as 40 different groupings. He tackles topics like Hindu marriage, why Hindus historically distrusted Muslims, or why he believed the Hindu upper class were *monists* (believing in one unified divine force over all). His work on calendars included the religious calendars of Jews, Christians, Zoroastrians, and Sogdians. He also attempted to objectively study the Jewish, Zoroastrian and Christian religions, producing treaties on these groups, which have not survived. Following in his footsteps was another Muslim scholar, Al-Shahrastani (1086-1153 CE) who assembled an impressive body of work entitled *Kitāb al–Milal wa al-Nihal* (The Book of Sects and Creeds) detailing his understanding of the religions of the world. His study identified sects within religions, which he endeavored to describe in a non-polemical (unbiased) fashion.

Conquest, Refutation, Conversion

Certain medieval Christians like Peter the Venerable (1092-1156) had studied the religion of Islam, but mainly in order to refute it. In 1141 Peter journeyed to Spain in order to have access to copies of the Islamic sources. He was in fact responsible for collecting a number of Islamic works that he later had translated into Latin. Peter commissioned Robert of Ketton and Hermann of Dalmatia to prepare Latin translations of the sacred *Quran* and other Muslim doctrinal works. They also translated materials from the *Hadith* relating to the life of the Prophet Muhammad.[2] This particular case of Christian interest in the scriptures of Islam was an area that I investigated as a young scholar with work that I was doing on St. Bernard of Clairvaux (1090-1153). Bernard, who had heard about Peter's project was said to have encouraged the translations.[3] In 1143, Peter the Venerable had asked Bernard, the esteemed Cistercian abbot of Clairvaux, to write a commentary on the Quran. Peter's goal was not only that Christians might come to an understanding of Islamic thought, but to do so in the hope that they might be better able to refute it. Peter wrote to Bernard:

> *In having this translation prepared, my intention was to follow the precedent set by the Church Fathers who never at any time let slip the opportunity of refuting even the most absurd heresy. Rather, they martialed all the strength of their faith to oppose it, and to demonstrate in their writings and disputations what a damnable and odious thing it was. And so I wanted to do the same with respect especially to this error of errors, so that the uninformed, by recognizing how it has with its deadly pestilence infected half of the world, may recognize its stupid and disgusting nature and see therefore how execrable and despicable it is.*[4]

Shortly after he returned from Spain, Peter again petitioned Bernard to compose arguments against some of the newly translated Islamic literature (these surviving translations are now become better known as the *Toledan Collection*). Peter wrote to the Cistercian abbot:

> *I had translated from Arabic into the Latin language also all the unholy sectarian doctrine, the life of the nefarious man (Muhammad), and the law which is called the Koran ... I have made all these things known to you especially, that I may*

communicate our zealous studies to such a friend, and that I may animate that magnificent learning of yours, which God has so singularly granted to you in our days, to write against so pernicious an error ... This task is yours ... Therefore if there is, by the inspiration of God, any willingness on the part of your reverence to work on these things, for the ability will not fail to be there through His Grace, reply ... that through your mouth, filled with the praise of Him, the benign Spirit may reply to the spirit of iniquity, and fill up the treasures of his Church with the wealth of your wisdom.[5]

There has been much debate as to Peter's actual motives in studying Islamic literature. He may have done so as a means to refute Islamic teachings or to peacefully persuade Muslims to accept the message of Christianity. Later on, Peter's disappointment over Western Christian indifference to any sort of Islamic dialogue may well have been directed toward St. Bernard. For it is likely that Bernard never replied to Peter's letter of 1143 concerning the composition of a critique for the translated Islamic teachings. At least, there exists no record of Bernard's attempt to compose such a refutation of the works of Islam.[6] Bernard's silence on the matter may be indicative of an attitude which saw the hopelessness of a Christian / Islamic dialogue as well any practical potential conversion of various Muslim people.

An example that demonstrates religious studies aimed at attempts toward a desire for conversion and conquest comes again from medieval Christian scholars, and aimed again at Islam. Toward the end of the Crusading period, a Franciscan friar, Raymond Lull (1232-1316) came up with a plan to bring missionary efforts to the Islam, which he believed would result in a peaceful conquest. In his *Book of Contemplation on God*, Lull wrote:

> *It is my belief, O Christ, that the conquest of the Holy Land should be attempted in no other way than as Thou and Thy apostles undertook to accomplish it – by love, by prayer, by tears, and the offering up of our own lives.*[7]

Lull has studied Jewish and Muslim mysticism and entered into public debates with Jewish scholars and rabbis on theological topics. He spent 9 years studying the Arabic language and Islamic literature in order to bolster his Christian apologetical position. He planned to use the tools of logic and philosophy in debate and had prepared an extensive series of questions and answers that he had would draw from in his discussions. Lull even bought had a Muslim slave for the explicit purpose of assisting him with linguistics. He traveled about Europe for a number of years promoting his conquest through conversion plan. In 1292, he was sent to Tunis where (in Arabic) he engaged in a number of public debates with Muslim scholars. He was later imprisoned and sent back to Europe. Some 15 years later (in 1308) he traveled to Burgia, Algeria where he proceeded to publicly teach Christianity in the city square. He was attacked, imprisoned and after 6 months sent home. In 1311, after much prompting from Lull, the Council of Vienna determined it was in the interest of Christianity to teach Jewish and Islamic language and literature at all the papal schools along with the universities of Paris, Salamanca, Oxford. At the age of 82, Lull made one more missionary trip back to Algeria. He worked there for almost a year among a small group of converts. During a public speech in the marketplace he was grabbed and taken to a place outside the city of Burgia where he was stoned. He died shortly thereafter. Some 265 works are attributed to this scholar.

During the ages of expansion and discovery of the 15th through 17th centuries there are numerous accounts of explorers who came into contact with other cultures and their indigenous religions. Chaplains assigned to these expeditions often gave fairly accurate descriptions of native religious practice and sought to learn more about their beliefs to assist in missionary efforts. Believing their cultures superior and that their religion would provide eternal salvation studies of native culture and religion were justified. A good example comes from the Spanish missionary Fr. Ramon Pane, one of the 5 chaplains on Columbus' 2nd expedition (1493-1496). Columbus instructed Pane to investigate and record accounts of religious practices of the native Taino on the island of Hispaniola (now Haiti and the Dominican Republic). The men he had left there from his first voyage had all been killed. Fr. Ramon produced detailed ethnographic accounts of the Taino including all the religious practices he had witnessed on the island. Information about gods (zemis), rituals, ceremonial objects, interaction with spirits, roles of the priests and the kings (caciques), views of afterlife, were included in his meticulous records. His collection of information was later published by Columbus' son Ferdinand under the title *Historie*.[8] There is some record of missionary effort attempted by Columbus' clerics among the Taino and much information about subsequent delegations of missionaries were sent by the Franciscans to Hispaniola well into the early 1500's. The city of Santo Domingo on the island eventually became the center of Christian directives for all of New Spain.

Desire for Harmony and Unity

In the twelfth century, English philosopher, linguist, and Franciscan friar, Roger Bacon (1220-1292), began an investigation of theological and philosophical principles of other faiths. The German philosopher and theologian Nicholas of Cusa (1401-1464) wrote *De Pace Fidei* (On the Peace of Faith), which was an imaginary description of a meeting in Heaven of 17 of the leading political and religious leaders of his day (Latin Christians, Eastern Christians, Middle Eastern Rite Christians, a Hindu from India, a Tartar, various Jews and Muslims). The participants, through reason, after meeting with God, the angels, St. Peter, and St. Paul, come to an agreement that there would be a single religion with the various groups having their own rites. While much of the description is decidedly Christian, interests of the other groups are respected. He does however mention that Jews might ultimately break from the union at some point. Nicholas also wrote *Cribratio Alchorani* (Sifting the Quran), which was a Latin review and translation of the Quran. Least we think Nicholas and other medieval Christians were on their way to some literal form of tolerance and unity among religions, it was Nicholas' 1451 order that forced Jews of the Dutch city of Arnhem to wear badges that identified them.

One of the great examples of sharing knowledge among and about the various faith traditions came from the court of the

Indian Mughul Emperor Akbar (1542-1605). He invited within his imperial circles representatives from the major faiths (Christian, Hindu, Buddhist, Jain, Zoroastrian) in addition to his own Muslim advisors. Theologians, poets, philosophers, scholars and religious leaders were invited to court in order to dialogue about faith. Drawing upon Sufi (Islamic mystical) principles Akbar even proposed a new unified state religion, *Din-i-ilahi* (the religion of God). In doing so he moved the Mughul court away from its traditional domination by Muslim clerics. He allowed Hindus and Jains to publicly worship and even helped rebuild their temples that had been destroyed by previous Muslim rulers. He sponsored translations of Hindu religious literature into Persian and attended Hindu festivals. He even had his son Maurad taught lessons from the New Testament. Akbar's library was said to have comprised some 24,000 volumes including Persian, Hindi, Greek, Latin, Arabic, and Kashmir texts. Yet he, himself, never learned to read or write. The Ibidat Khana (house of worship) in Fategpur Sikri, built in 1575, was turned into a place of interfaith dialogue after debates among the Sunni who were using the space turned virulent. Historian Muhammad Abdul Baki (1611-1688) wrote of Akbar: *"he would recognize no difference between religions, his object being to unite all men in a common bond of peace"*. He was a proponent of *Suleh-i-Kul* (universal toleration). In a letter sent to King Phillip II of Spain in 1582, Akbar stated that he associated with *"learned men of all religions, thus depriving profit from their exquisite discourses and exalted aspirations."* He went on to say that far too many people blindly *"follow the religion in which they were born and educated, thus excluding themselves from the possibility of ascertaining the truth, which is the noblest aim of the human intellect."* Akbar invited individuals to open their minds to understanding that was outside of their own traditions, suggesting that no one faith or religion had a complete grasp of truth.[9]

Intellectual Interest

During the later period of world discovery, as Europeans set out on boats to explore other continents Christian, thinkers began to move beyond the medieval practice of critiquing other monotheistic faith (Judaism and Islam) along with an across the board discounting of polytheism. As chaplains who accompanied voyages began to report back about the strange religious practices they encountered in the Americas, Africa and Asia, an interest in these practices began to develop. Jesuit missionaries in China translated various works of Confucius into Latin. In fact one of his works (*Lunyu*) is still referred to as the *Analects* in English from the name of the 17th century Latin translation entitled *Analectus*.

What inevitably turned the corner toward the critical study of religion was the use of scientific and philosophical methods of inquiry. We will deal with the sequence of these events that prompted these influences in our next chapter. The intellectual ferment throughout Europe in the last three quarters of 1800's was responsible for fostering new approaches to investigating the social sciences, philosophy, theology, sacred scriptures, and various disciplines in the humanities. As disciplines began to collide, collapse, and overlap social scientists began to look more closely at the religious practices, behaviors, and organized activities of certain groups. Colonialism, European expansion, trade, and conquest had much to do with this. Interest in the activities of persons outside both the contemporary and historical Judeo-Christian mainstream brought about a scientific and scholarly study of cultures and their approaches to seeking the meaning of life or sources and principles that governed their world. This coupled with changes of attitudes about cultures and religions would move scholars toward more open dialogue.

1. *Tarikh Al-Hindi*, Vol 1 (1910) in E. Sachau, ed., *Al-Beruni's India: an Account of the Religion, Philosophy, Literature, Geography, Chronology, Astronomy, Customs, Laws and Astrology of Indiae*, London: Kegan Paul, Trench, Trubner & Co. See also Ahmed Hasan Dani, *Alberuni's Indica: A record of the cultural history of South Asia about AD 1030*, University of Islamabad Press *(1973)* and "The Forefather of Religious Studies" (2015)

2. Penny J. Cole, "The Theme of Religious Pollution In Crusade Documents", M. Shatz Miller ed., *Crusaders and Muslims in Twelfth-Century Syria* (Leiden: E.J. Brill, 1993), p. 102.

3. James Kritzeck, *Peter the Venerable and Islam* (Princeton University Press, 1964), p. 22.

4. Giles Constable (ed.), *The Letters of Peter the Venerable*, pp. 294-5.

5. Giles Constable (ed.), *The Letters of Peter the Venerable*, pp. 294-5. The translations commissioned by Peter were: *Masa 'il Abi-al-Harith* by *'Abdillah iban-Salam, Kitab Nasab Rasul Allah* by Sa'id ibn-Umar, a *Life* of the Prophet Muhammad and the Ouran.

6. Tim Davis, St. Bernard of Clairvaux: A Monastic View of medieval Violence (1998), p.179.

7. Raymond Lull, "Book of Contemplation on God", in *Raymon Llull and the Secret Life*, Amador Vega, trans. James W. Heisig (2002)

8. A complete translation of Fr. Ramon's collection appears in Edward Gaylord Bourne's *Columbus, Ramon Pane and the Beginnings of American Anthropology*, (1906)

9. Craig Considine, "Finding Tolerance in Akbar, the Philosopher-King" (2013).

2

Refining Academic Approaches

Early Influences

The 16th century saw a turning point in the evolution of religious inquiry. Significant were the origins of the Protestant Reformation early in that century, coupled with later changes in the way that nature and existence of God were perceived by European philosophers and scientists. Both had profound effects on the religious landscape. In the late 1500's and early 1600's, with discoveries by astronomers like Copernicus, Kepler, and Galileo, questions were raised as to how we should understand our place in the universe. If the Church were to adopt the idea that the earth was in motion (no longer motionless and at the center of the cosmos), then the revealed word of God as transmitted to humanity in the Bible would be contradicted.[1] Furthermore, if scientific knowledge of the regions above the earth led us to believe in infinitely distant moving stars and planets, it might bring us to begin to ask unsettling theological questions. Exactly where was heaven, and ultimately, where did God reside? So many issues caused traditional views of God and the Judeo-Christian faith to be re-examined. Some philosophers tried to arrive at logical conclusions, others sought to expand the definition of God. Hindus in the Post-Classical period, when faced with some of the same questions regarding ultimacy, looked toward logical, practical, and even mystical connections between what we know and the mystery that remains beyond. The Jewish philosopher Benedict Spinoza (1632-1677) went so far as to suggest that nature <u>was</u> God. Spinoza believed that God did not exist outside nature. He said, whatever exists, exists in God, who is the sum total of all. Almost a century later, the philosopher Immanuel Kant (1724-1804) was at the forefront of philosophical leanings toward agnosticism (not knowing if God exists). While the term "agnosticism" was not coined until 1869, Kant suggested that because of the limitations of argumentation and in the absence of irrefutable evidence, no one could really know whether there is a God, or an afterlife. For the sake of morality and as a ground for reason, Kant asserted, people are justified in believing in God, even though they could never be certain of God's existence empirically. The work of philosophers who would follow, like Hegel, Feuerbach, and Nietzsche, created more skepticism about our interpretations of the traditional monotheistic God, which eventually moved the critical study of Christianity and criticisms of other world religions, at least in certain circles, toward a more balanced footing. However, when it came to understanding and appreciating the beliefs of those who were outside their own faith, for the majority of western monotheists, this was still a large stretch. The value of looking for truths in other religions, or learning about their objects of devotion would continue to be something that was seriously questioned. Yet, when it came to truths, at this time there were some average Christians who began to question certain literal teachings (Adam and Eve, Noah, some biblical miracles) within their own traditions.

In the 17th century, we began to see philological (relationship of language) studies for ancient and biblical texts. Historical investigations of cultures mentioned in the bible along with their literature became common in academic circles. As early as 1617, the English scholar John Selden wrote a book entitled *De diis Syriss* (*On the Syrian Gods*), which looked at the Semitic deities, mentioned in the Old Testament of the Bible. A later work by John Spencer (*De Legibus Hebraeorum Ritualibus Et Earum Rationalibus Libri Tres*) constituted a three-volume attempt to root the religious activities of Israel in those earlier ancient cultures that surrounded them. This type of scholarship continued into the 1700's with the development of new approaches to categorize and analyze religion. German philologists Christian Heyne (1729-1812) and Johann Eichorn (1753-1737) began to study the notion of myths, seeing their appearance in biblical narratives along with the problem of defining the concept of "religion". Abraham Anquetil-Duperron explored the religions of India in the mid 1700's while traveling through the subcontinent and in 1771 published a 3-volume work of Zoroastrian scriptures. One of the more famous European scholars to work outside his own tradition was Sir William Jones (sometimes known as Oriental Jones), who was a British judge in India. Knowledgeable of Sanskrit, he postulated the theory of Indo-European languages along the way making comparisons of the Greek and Roman gods with those of the Hindus. Jones was also involved with scholars who translated the Hindu Sanskrit scriptures into English.

Greater Openness Among Academics in the 1800's

As fields of inquiry in modern academic disciplines began to broaden, the *world's religions* began to be investigated as type of social science. This was likely in motion by 1820 and was most noticeable in the work of European scholars, some of it even effecting the ideological direction of their universities. Roughly 20 years earlier, Western scholars had succeeded in naming and cataloguing most of the major world religions.[2] At first, these investigations were done by scholars in a less than open-minded fashion, mostly in deference to their own Christian faith, which they believed to be more evolved and superior. One of the key figures in securing the gap between the modern study of religion along the philosophical and theological frontiers of European scholarship was Friedrich Max Mueller (1823-1900). He was a philologist (expert in languages) whose familiarity with Sanskrit, Arabic, and Persian facilitated developments in scientific methods of linguistic and textual study. He believed that studying and understanding languages within their proper cultural and historical setting allowed for greater contextualization of meaning and intent. (As opposed to merely translating and trying to apply modern meanings to the texts.) Many of his methods began to be used in the historical-critical study of the Judeo-Christian scriptures, as we will see later in this chapter, but also in investigating other world scriptures and literature. Mueller also dabbled in psychological linguistic theories about the primitive human mind. Along with William Jones, Mueller was an advocate of the theory that many of the early gods were those who were connected to forces of nature.

Mueller believed that one of the basic human feelings that made people religious was their helplessness before forces more powerful than themselves. Thus, the powers of nature were given names, and these names were eventually projected upon gods who controlled (or were) nature.[3] Mueller posited that humans "invented" the gods out of a need to give us some feeling of recourse or control. If the gods were anthropomorphic (having human qualities) humans might pray and appeal to them for their help, if they shared elements of our common nature. In the 1830's more works on non-Christian religions began to appear in connection to the presence and influence of the British East India Company. In 1827 a German biblical scholar named Wilhelm deWette wrote a book entitled *Religion: Its Nature, the Forms in Which It Appears, and Its Influence on Life*. At this time philosophers like Hegel and Schopenhauer began to take into account notions within the Asian religions when constructing their philosophical word views.

Other open-minded scholars increasingly became interested in the pursuit of cataloguing religions. Hannah Adams (1755-1831) was one of the first American women to be able to support herself solely by writing. Around 1820, influenced by Christian denominational controversies and disagreements in Massachusetts, she took up an interest in studying about religions of the world. Her inspiration came from a 2-volume work by a British scholar, Thomas Broughton, entitled *A Historical Dictionary of All Religions from the Creation of the World to this Present Time.* The work of course condemned all non-Christian and Jewish groups as being inaccurate, but it spurred Adams, then a Congregationalist, to begin assembling notes for what would be her more open-minded approach to the topic. Adam's *An Alphabetical Compendium of the Various Sects Which Have Appeared from the Beginning of the Christian Era to the Present Day,* was published in 1784. An updated edition entitled *A View of Religions* was printed in 1791, and several subsequent works including *A Dictionary of All Religions and Religious Denominations* followed.

Editions and revisions continued through 1820. These works all claimed to have been written with an intentionally objective viewpoint. However, Adam's objectivity was far from complete and much of her understanding was distorted, if not simply uncharitable. She regularly classified Catholics as Papists, polytheists as Heathens and concluded that the most pervasive practice of paganism involved worship of the Dalai Lama. Nonetheless, this was the very first American work to attempt an exhaustive survey of the world's religions. Later in life described herself as someone who had come to adopt the Unitarian (God as a single entity, non-Trinitarian, Jesus was a human being). In 1815, Thomas Williams, an English writer, took Adams research and added to it substantially, creating an alphabetically arranged work entitled *A Dictionary of All Religions*.

By the 1820's the academic study of religion was beginning to be launched in Europe, and would lag by few decades in the Americas. But popularly directed works of a more apological nature also began to proliferate. Apological works for Christian missionaries that were produced at this time critically addressed the idolatrous nature of non-Christian traditions. The United States had their share of these circles. Even certain academic works for use in higher education continued to contain a tone of superiority when referring to Christianity. Prejudices, judgements, and opinions all rang through. James Moffat (1811-1890), a scholar of the new historical-critical method wrote about comparative religious study in 1852:

> *The various shades of philanthropy may be traced from nation to nation, by the corresponding degrees of Christian knowledge. From the midnight-blackness of Hindooism, through Mohammedanism, and Romanism, and formal Protestantism, to the humble, intelligent and faithful follower of the Word of God, you may distinctly grade the ascending scale of humanity.*[4]

Early breakthroughs among the more liberal Protestant groups in terms of increasingly open-minded treatment of non-

Christian faiths began in the early 1820's in the northeastern United States, particularly around Boston. It had recently become a trading center with India. This openness toward Asian religious ideas was especially true among Unitarians (as we saw with Hannah Adams), because elements of anti-Trinitarian attitudes were woven through their belief. It also opened the door for movements like the Transcendentalists, which we will discuss later. The Massachusetts Historical Association even went so far as to elect Sanskrit scholar Sir William (Oriental) Jones, who we previously mentioned, as a member. When Jones was living in India, Harvard had requested that he send them Sanskrit manuscripts for their library.[5] In 1871, James Freeman Clark published the work *Ten Great Religions*. This was followed in 1872 by Samuel Johnson's three-part study *Oriental Religions* and James Moffat's (then a professor at Princeton) *A Comparative History of Religion*. It is interesting to note the Moffat's view toward non-Christian religions became much less judgmental and harsh as he advanced in wisdom and age. Concerning the literary study of world scriptures, he wrote:

Advancements in the philosophical field of epistemology paved the way toward an intellectual openness and curiosity when it came to belief systems outside one's own experience. Interdisciplinary approaches to scholarship were another contributing factor.[6]

Influences of Evolutionary Theories upon The Study of Religion

As we have previously mentioned, in the mid 1800's and early 1900's interest in studying primitive cultures and their religious practices heightened, particularly among anthropologists from nations with colonial possessions. With impetus from Darwinian theories, anthropologists sought to map out the evolution of religious thought and practice. Most of these individuals were theists (believers in God). Also remember that these were mostly white European men who believed their cultures and religion to be superior to those in regions of the globe that were "developing". Theories in the phases of the religious progression of humanity proposed by the anthropologists were initially influenced by evolutionary scientific theories. They tried to explain the stages of progression in human understanding of the divine. Unfortunately, a number of these early anthropologists made critical mistakes in interpreting the ritual practice of native inhabitants. Theorists judged the religions of those they were observing to be primitive and surmised that their modes of worship had not advanced much since antiquity. They also attempted to compare their practices to what they knew about ancient religious activities. Scholars also thought they might detect common evolutionary patterns among geographically diverse peoples. A whole host of theoretical scenarios ensued, many of which were not in agreement. Just because they observed certain religious activity in what they perceived to be the world's most primitive cultures, it did not mean that the world's ancient cultures were actually involved in those same specific practices. Also, just because the evolution of religious practices was observed to be true in one primitive culture, did not mean that evolution could apply to all cultures.

E.B. Tylor (1832-1917) was an early English anthropologist who felt that *animism* (the notion that supernatural spirits or souls were behind all apparently living things) was the earliest religious expression. From there he believed that *polytheism* (belief in many gods) was the next natural progression as these spirits were themselves raised to more powerful supernatural beings who could act upon the world. Tylor believed that perceptions of hierarchy in the divine realm were patterned after perception of human government. He writes: *Among nation after nation it is still clear how, man being the type of deity, human society and government became the model on which divine society and government were shaped.*[7] Eventually Tylor came to believe these many gods merged into a unified power that tied all of these spiritual elements together, resulting in the practice of *monotheistic* worship. There were even two scholars, Andrew

Lang (1844-1912) and Fr. Wilhelm Schmidt, who believed monotheism to be the original belief (in some part based upon the Bible) and that polytheism and animism were corrupted expressions that emerged later.

Max Mueller (1823-1900) believed that our early ancestors first worshipped the elements of nature out of feelings of fear and awe, but later personified those forces and made them deities. Theories of psychological, evolutionary, and sensory elements that gave rise to religious expressions continued to surface in the early 1800's through the early 1900's. John Lubbock (1834-1913) believed the first stage of religious development in humanity was one of *atheism* (as early humans were of such little intelligence they were not able to perceive of God). He believed that societies next moved toward *fetishism* (using sacred objects that contained certain powers in religious ritual), then *nature worship*, later moving to *shamanism* (calling for an increased need for intermediaries between the human world and abode of the divine, which was now perceived to be far away). The last 2 stages involved *anthropomorphism* (gods with human-like characteristics, residing in nature, but represented to humans in images or idols) and *monotheism* (belief in a single deity who is the author of all life, nature, and morality). F.B. Jevons in his 1896 *Introduction to the History of Religion* wrote that religion began from *totemistic* (powerful religious symbols particular to a specific clan linking their relationship with the world of spirit/nature/divine) and *animistic* roots, then proceeded to *polytheism* and *monotheism*. Many European religious scholars of the 1800's misunderstood the concept of totemism believing it to be associated with religious foods and tribal sexual taboos. Scottish anthropologist John Ferguson McLennan wrote in 1869 that *"there is no race of men that has not come through this [totemistic] primitive stage of speculative belief"*.[8]

James Frazer (1854-1941) worked on ritual, myth and ethnographic material. One of his early theories was that ancient religions were highly connected to fertility cults that often involved worship of their king. He saw magic as one of the earliest religious practices, even categorizing various types of activity associated with ritual magic. The death and resurrection of sacred figures was also an area of his interest. Frazer believed that societies evolved from the age of magic, to one of religion, to one that ultimately would be replaced by science. Many of his early contributions came in comparative studies of ancient culture, myth and rites, which included corresponding observations in the history of Christianity. His seminal 12-volume work, *The Golden Bough*, is still part of the scholarly canon of mythology studies today. Unlike other anthropologists Frazer did not have much field experience with the primitive societies of his day but he did send surveys to missionary groups and colonial offices all over the world and assembled an important collection of death myths.

Arnold van Gannep (1873-1957) contributed greatly to theories on rites of passage, particularly the concept of "liminality". His work involved the transformative notions in various categories of rites (both religious and social) particularly within strictly prescribed rites of initiation. In his studies, connections were made between tribal and modern rites.

Liberal Protestant Theology and the Historical–Critical Method of Studying Sacred Scripture

When I was a young professor my family and I moved into an old house on the outskirts of Columbus (OH), sort of out in the country, in a serene setting, across from a horse farm. The area was just then beginning to be exploited by new (and expensive) housing developments. This was a prime target for the Jehovah's Witnesses. It was just days after we moved in (they watch the flow of the real estate market) that some local brothers and sisters visited us. My wife, busy with her own job, kids, and the new move, quickly brushed them off by indicating that her husband was a college religion professor and if they thought they were going to convert us they had better send the head of their community. (Working in corporate America my wife figured the head of anything would never take the time to personally attend to a task.)

The following week, one of the elders of the local kingdom hall rang our doorbell. Luckily I was home at the time (my wife may not have been so welcoming) and invited the gentleman in. After some discussion, he asked if I would be interested in meeting with him to learn more about the Bible and their beliefs. To his surprise (I think), I indicated that I knew very little about the Witnesses and if I was going to teach my students about the movement, what better way to learn than from one of their own elders. We began meeting on a regular basis and he was pleasantly surprised to find that after discussing a number of historical and theological topics, I was in agreement with a number of their beliefs. I truly learned a lot from these encounters and was grateful for the opportunity. However, when it came to the study of the scriptures, we were not able to find much common ground. The sticking point was the fact that every time we opened and read the Bible my theological training kicked in and I was completely unable to read or think about a passage of scripture without using the techniques of the historical-critical method that had become ingrained in my approach to sacred texts. The Witnesses are by no stretch fundamentalists but are taught their own techniques for interpreting the scriptures (some of which are historical-critical). They believe the scriptures are the inspired word of God, that they should be read and interpreted on their own, and that the scriptures stand on their own. The Witnesses use their own translation of the Bible (the New World Translation), which is not substantially different from commonly used academic versions. Certain words and passages are uniquely translated. A few of their doctrinal conclusions, while interesting, were not personally compelling for me. We agreed to disagree at that point, and after about a year or so, our studies ended. However, that very same elder continues to stop by every so often. We have been friends now for some 20 years and occasionally he will even be invited to visit my classes to give presentations on what Jehovah's Witnesses believe.

The point of the preceding story is that the Historical-Critical method (sometimes known as Higher Criticism) for interpreting scripture has become the standard in mainline to liberal academia for over 50 years. It actually began in the early to mid 1800's in Europe (as we have previously mentioned) rooted mainly in German scholarship and methodology in the *Religionsgeschichtliche Schule* (History of Religions School) during the period of change that drastically affected western academia. The Historical-Critical method (or Critical-Historical method) sees sacred scripture as a collection of documents written or collected by persons of faith. It asks questions like: when was this text written, where was it written, and who wrote it (if we can even know that for sure). The method goes on to investigate what was happening socially, politically and historically at the time, what might have influenced the writer, and to what audience might he be addressing his work. Obviously, the writer could be female, although this was almost always not the case. Of additional concern would be the sources used by the author. Were these originally oral sources, and were there other possible written versions? While such studies began with Jewish and Christian works, Historical Criticism has been used to interpret Hindu and

Buddhist texts, the Quran and various versions of Confucian tradition.

One of the fathers of the historical-critical approach actually began writing in the 18th century, a biblical scholar named Hermann Reimarus (1694-1768). He was a Deist who believed that God had created the universe, set it into motion, created the laws of nature, and from that point on the world operated solely on the causalities understood by science. Remarus thought that humans, through reason and the study of nature, could arrive at some knowledge of God on their own as well as some understanding of morality. God did not intervene in human affairs through miracles or the incarnation of a son. He therefore did not believe in the divinity of Jesus but as a result began to embark on a critical study of Jesus as a mortal Jewish teacher and apocalyptic prophet. Much of his more controversial work remained unpublished but he did start scholars in the direction of critical biblical thought.

Another early founder was linguistics scholar Johann Gottfried Eichhorn (1752-1827). In studying the Hebrew scriptures, he came to realize that the contemporary translations had passed through far too many hands and that some of the miraculous events described in both Jewish and Christian scriptures could in fact be explained by natural causes. He looked to interpret them from the viewpoint of the ancient world instead of his own society. Lastly, he observed that a number of the letters of Paul were probably not written by him (which is still believed by scholars today).

Ferdinand Christian Bauer (1792-1860) of the Tubingen School of Theology introduced the Higher Criticism notion of the differences between Jewish and Gentile Christianity. Adolph von Harnack contributed to the liberal atmosphere of the academy investigating the Greek philosophical roots and pagan influences upon Christianity. There were no topics too controversial for his seminars. He criticized the historical validity of the Gospel of John and suggested that certain miracles of Jesus may actually have only seemed miraculous.

Linked to historical-critical study was the work of Liberal Protestant Theology that gripped European schools during the same time period. Albrecht Ritschl (1822-1889) is often associated with the liberal perspective that came out of Germany in the mid-1800's. Influenced by the philosophy of Immanuel Kant, he attempted to separate Christianity from science by suggesting that scientific truths were judgements of fact while religious truths were judgements of value.[9] For Ritschl, religion was rooted in the everyday expressions of love and moral action that was not necessarily "other-worldly", but grounded in reason and practical application. He believed that Jesus' essence (before he came to earth) was not that of an earthly body in a heavenly realm, but maybe some sort of presence or idea in the mind of God. For Ritschl, Jesus was a man, and we should focus on his life and teachings, which will lead us to God. In this way, like the philosopher Schleiermacher (1768-1834), Ritschl's view of reality did not contradict science. Traditional Christian ideas like miracles, angels, devils, heaven, hell, virgin birth and the second coming were all relegated by him to the realm of medieval thinking. As liberal theologians began to take control of major Protestant seminaries, those scholars who held out for the factual reality of parting seas, and water changing into wine, were eventually shown the door. The scriptures were a matter of interpretation and inspiration. No longer would persons with contradictory theological views suffer torture, or death by fire at the stake. In 1873, Friedrich Max Muller, an Oxford professor fluent in Sanskrit rolled out his *Introduction to the Science of Religion,* which became the cornerstone of modern comparative religious studies. Several years later, Cornelius P. Tiele started teaching courses in the History of Religions at the University of Leiden. American contributions such as Unitarian James Freeman Clarke's *Ten Great Religions* made less of a splash on the academic scene.

One of the best examples of an early discovery in Higher Criticism from the Christian tradition resulted in the development of the idea of what has become the current understanding of the Synoptic Gospels (Mark, Matthew and Luke, which are often studied together in seminary curricula). Up until the early 1800's it was believed that Matthew was the oldest Gospel (that's why we often list them as Matthew, Mark, Luke and John). Using Literary Criticism, scholars discovered that Luke and Matthew were using Mark as a source, and almost completely incorporate it into their texts. There are also groups of sayings of Jesus (that we still need to know more about) and miracle stories were in use at the time. These factor into our interpretation. John was using additional and possibly different sources, and wrote from a different point of view. About 90% of the material in John is not paralleled in the other Gospels. Some of the chronology, geography, and settings are different. John's Gospel is highly symbolic and uses dualistic language (above and below, truth and lies, light and darkness) to depict the separation between good and evil. The dynamic between the author and audience is an important nuance. From this information, we might be able to further understand more explicit purposes that the writer had for producing the text. Lastly the method looks at the text in its historical context and attempts to refrain from imposing modern agendas, individual bias by the interpreter (although, as we will see in one of the next sections this is sometimes difficult), as well as taking into account linguistic and cultural differences. There are 5 basic methodologies used in the critical method: Source Criticism, Redaction Criticism, Form Criticism, Tradition Criticism and Canonical Criticism. We will briefly look at each along with their origin and evolving influence.

Form Criticism attempts to look at literary patterns within the scriptures and to trace back different forms to earlier oral traditions. It is interested in getting back to the original forms of information or looking at genre (was it a parable story, a saying, a poem, a letter, a proverb). Form criticism looks for the real-life situation or *Sitz im Leben*, in its cultural and sociological setting. It then asks how these pericopes (sets of verses) or literary constructs of thought fit into the purpose or theme of the entire text of scripture. The original developers of the method focused mainly on the Hebrew Scriptures. This school consisted of famous theologians such as Hermann Gunkel (1862-1932), Martin Dibelius (1883-1947), Gerhard von Rad (1901-1971), and Rudolf Bultmann (1884-1976). Many scholars went on to apply methods originally used in Old Testament works to the Christian Gospels. Bultmann was also interested in demythologizing the texts, not by completely doing away with myth, but by using the genre of myth to get to the symbolic kernel of truth that the writer really wanted to address. He saw the historical Jesus as a mixture of history and myth. In order to find any truth beyond that we have to penetrate and understand the mythical setting that comes both before and afterward.

Source Criticism evaluates sources of information both within and outside the scripture. The German historian Leopold von Ranke (1795-1886) was at the forefront of its use. His insistence on relying upon primary sources (those closest to the event such as eyewitnesses, original documents, diaries, government documents, memoirs) had a tremendous impact on the evolution of the historical method in numerous fields of study. Numerous independent sources that contain the same information strengthen credibility. Seeing how particular motivations of source writers might produce some sort of bias. Julius Wellhausen (1844-1918) is one of the best-known biblical scholars for implementing Source Criticism in the discipline of religious studies. His work ranged from the investigation of Hebrew scriptures to both Christian and Islamic works. Wellhausen is often praised for his work on the Documentary Hypothesis of the Torah (first 5 books of the Hebrew scriptures). The Documentary Hypothesis, which is still in wide use today, suggests that the first 5 books of the Hebrew Bible (once attributed to Moses) were compiled from at least 4 different historical periods, written by numerous authors. He believed that the document was not written in historical order but in layers that were patched together later on to form a historical narrative. Language and perspectives within the text were linked to the various stages of Israel's history and not necessarily consistent with accounts written at the time of the events. Late 20th century scholars have expanded and tweaked this interpretation to include additional editors and collectors of independent narratives, which were brought together in various stages of the editorial process.

Redaction criticism views the author of scriptural texts as more of an "editor" or redactor who uses his various sources to achieve a narrative that expresses certain theological opinions and points of view relative to the community being addressed at that time. Chroniclers might have been more concerned with their own theological agenda rather than historical accuracy and facts. Gunther Bornkamm (1905-1990) was one of the scholars responsible for the popularity of redaction criticism. He also did second generation work on the Quest for the Historical Jesus, following the work of Albert Schweitzer. Hans Conselmann (1915-1989), also a redaction critic who looked at the Gospel of Luke and how the author shifted Jesus' message from one of expectation for the Messiah's return and the eschaton (end times and final events) to a larger picture of the work of Jesus in history, including the work of the kingdom in the Mediterranean Roman Empire at the time.

Tradition Criticism is often associated with biblical scholar Hermann Gunkel (1862-1932) and examines the traditions behind the writing. Gunkel was part of the school of thought that saw the origins of ancient Hebrew sacred literature influenced by traditions from other Near Eastern religions in Mesopotamia and Egypt. He believed this began with oral traditions and extended to the written literature itself. By examining and comparing similarities in the narratives of certain early Hebrew scripture stories with those of their polytheistic neighbors he saw numerous parallels. Later he extended his comparisons to the New Testament literature. Tradition Criticism is used today in analysis of historical folklore.

Biblical Archaeology and Interest in Non-Monotheist Religions

Interest and advancements in the field of archaeology also served to bring together a greater awareness and appreciation of non-monotheistic religious traditions. Some of this began in earnest attempts to add to our knowledge of biblical literature and history by investigating the cultures mentioned in the Judeo-Christian scriptures that came into contact with "God's chosen people". Significant discoveries date from the mid 1800's. Some of the more influential developments in the field came from Flinders Petrie (1853-1942), an Egyptian archaeologist from Britain helped advance the field of Egyptology into a modern academic discipline by using scientifically precise recordings in dating the layers and pottery found in his excavations. Petrie is also credited with unearthing one of the most important finds for biblical archaeology in Egypt, the famous Merneptah Stele (a huge stone carved with detailed inscriptions from the reign of the Pharaoh Merneptah, discovered at Thebes in 1896). The stele archaeologically links Egypt with the Israelites, who Merneptah mentions he conquered in the early 1200's BCE. The evidence is priceless because it proves that early contact with Egypt by the Hebrews was much more than a story, and made historical dating of their encounter possible. Archaeological evidence of the Exodus is yet to be found, and may never be. Countless exhaustive attempts have come up empty. However, in the process, much was discovered of the Egyptians and a comparative interest in their religious activity is an important part of 19th century advancements in the early study of religion. Another example from this period of academic inquiry was Morris Jastrow (1861-1921) who was a professor of Semitic languages and a librarian at the University of Pennsylvania. In 1898, he wrote a 700-page book on *The Religion of Babylon and Assyria*. His father was a Talmudic scholar and rabbi. After becoming a rabbi himself, Morris left his ministry for a life devoted to scholarship. Archaeological investigation and curiosity about the link between these cultures and the ancient Hebrews made this work possible. In the years to follow, the University of Pennsylvania, along with the University of Chicago, would become leading centers of Near Eastern scholarship and contribute greatly to the emerging understanding of religion in the ancient cultures of Egypt, Sumer, Akkad, Babylon, Assyria, and Persia.

1. The idea that the earth was motionless (and did not revolve around the sun) followed a literal interpretation of the scriptures. See 1 Chronicles 16:30, Psalm 93:1, Psalm 96:10, Psalm 104:5, Ecclesiastes 1:5.

2. James Turner, *Religion Enters the Academy* (2011).

3. Ross Aden, *Religion Today: A Critical Approach to Religious Studies* (2013), p.40.

4. James Moffat, *An Address Delivered at the Opening of the Third Session of the Cincinnati Theological Seminary of the Presbyterian Church* (1852).

5. James Turner, *Religion Enters the Academy* (2011), p. 36.

6. James Moffat, *A Comparative History of Religion, Dodd & Meade* (1873).

7. Tylor, *Primitive Culture* (1871).

8. McLennan, *Fortnightly Review* (1869).

9. Roger Olson, *The Story of Christian Theology* (1999), p. 548.

3

Defining Religion

As we continue the investigation of religion(s) one might think it would be helpful to define exactly what constitutes a religion. Some would say it is a concept that is natural to humanity. Others might say it is a response to a divine reality or call. There are scholars who describe it as an idea that emerges from western culture, beliefs and philosophies. Clearly it is historical, and its activities are real, regardless of whether or not its object of attention is. Unfortunately, contemporary scholars have been unable to agree on any kind of general or succinct definition that fits all practices. One common problem is that many are unable to approach the study from a neutral perspective. We are always influenced by our own baggage from our upbringing in terms of what we were previously taught about our own traditions (or aversions toward traditions). For example, some Christians might say that Buddhism is not a religion because Buddhists do not worship a god. They do have rituals and prayer or meditation. Is Scientology a religion? They do believe in souls and the elevation of the human spirit. The Supreme Court gave Scientology tax status as a religion in 1993. Yet there is no ritual worship or divinity there either. Then in 2016 the court revoked Scientology's tax-exempt status saying it could operate as a business, but not a tax-exempt non-profit religious organization. The United Kingdom did not recognize Scientology as a religion until 2013.

Now, there are all kinds of other judgements made upon religions and denominations. When it comes to categorizing what qualifies as a Christian, certain Protestants might say that Catholics, Mormons, and Jehovah's Witnesses are not Christian, mainly because of the way Christianity is defined in their particular Protestant tradition, or simply because that is what they have been brought up to believe. Thus, when coming to study people of various faiths, our perception of what a religion is or what it should look like is colored by our own orientation or indoctrination. The personal, cultural, or societal viewpoint is frequently our starting place, and actually, probably should be. How else would we begin with a frame of reference? The same can be said for the orientation of scholars who each come to their study from a tradition (or sometimes lack thereof). Although in the field of the *study of religion*, scholars are trained to set aside (in as much as it is possible) beliefs that might impede critical thinking and understanding. They must trust in the fact that the gathering of information will lead them to a clearer perception of reality. Apologists (those arguing for controversial viewpoints) and advocates for particular religious teachings have traditionally taught adherents that anything outside their own sphere of doctrinal belief is really not "true" religion, but rather superstitious practices, the work of the devil, or misguided thinking. If they believe in divine revelation (which we will cover in another chapter), even the most open-minded of learners must opt for what they believe to be from God or the source of *ultimacy* (that which is perceived as supreme reality). We generally fall back on our own experiences (both good and bad) when making judgements of this kind.

As scholars began to develop academic approaches to the study of religion they proffered wide definitions of what might constitute religion. What follows is a sampling of definitions of religion or belief arranged in chronological order. They come from philosophers, theologians, and scholars of religion.

Immanuel Kant (1724-1804) said that *religion is about actions and practices* it is *the recognition of all our duties as divine commands*.

Friedrich Schleiermacher (1768-1834) - *a feeling for the infinite, and a feeling of absolute dependence.*

Georg Hegel (1770-1831) - *The knowledge possessed by the finite mind of its nature as absolute. Religion leads us to a Universal, which embraces all within itself, to an Absolute by which all else is* *brought into being: and this absolute is an object not of the senses but of mind and thought.*

Karl Marx (1818-1883) wrote: *man makes religion, religion does not make man... It is the imaginary realization of the human essence, because the human essence possesses no true reality.*

Marx was critical of religious oppression. He saw it as a tool of the aristocracy, industrialists, and capitalists. While religion could provide some comfort, it also became a crutch of the underclass and the working class. It was an illusory promise of hope in an afterlife that would be much better than their suffering in the present. In his *Critique of Hegel's Philosophy of Right,* Marx expressed the often-quoted phrase: *Religion is the moan of the oppressed creature, the sentiment of a heartless world, as it is the spirit of spiritless conditions. It is the opium of the people.*

F. Max Muller (1823-1900) in his 1891 *Lectures on the Origin and Growth of Religion,* said that faith was: *nothing more than ordinary consciousness developed and modified in such a way as* *to enable one to apprehend religious objects; that is, objects or beings which cannot be apprehended by sense or reason.* Accordingly, he defined religion as *the apprehension or perception of the infinite under various names or guises ... such an apprehension is the necessary condition for all historical religions for they all display a longing for the infinite ... without it, no religion, not even the lowest worship of idols and fetishes, would be possible; and if we will but listen attentively, we can hear in all religions a groaning of the spirit, a struggle to conceive the inconceivable.*

William James (1842-1919) in *The Varieties of Religious Experience* wrote: *Religion...shall mean for us the feelings, acts and experiences of individual men in their solitude, so as they apprehend themselves to stand in relation to whatever they may consider divine. Since relation may be either moral, physical, or ritual, it is evident that out of religion in the sense of which we take it, theologies, philosophies and ecclesiastical organizations may secondarily grow.* He also commented: *were one asked to* *characterize the life of religion in the broadest and most general terms possible, one might say that it consists of the belief that there is an unseen order, and that our supreme good lies in harmoniously adjusting ourselves thereto.* In a 1902 lecture James commented: *the very fact that there are so many, and so different from one another, is enough to prove that the word 'religion' cannot stand for any single principle or essence, but is rather a collective name.* And in *The Varieties...* he wrote: *the man who knows religion most completely troubles himself least about a definition.*

Sociologist **Emile Durkheim** (1858-1917) wrote: *A religion is a unified system of beliefs and practices relative to sacred things, that is to say, things set apart and forbidden - beliefs and practices which unite into one single moral community called a Church, all those who adhere to them.* In his groundbreaking *Elementary Forms of Religious Life* (1912) he investigated various theories of religion and examined the cultural and social aspects of religious phenomena among both indigenous and contemporary societies.

Durkheim saw religion as one of the most basic functions of society, which at an early stage in civilization was responsible for the cohesion of a community. He also suggested that human emotion was a primary factor in the religious experience, a response to a reality that was beyond our full comprehension.

Philosopher **Alfred North Whitehead** (1862-1947) in his *Religion in the Making* wrote: *Religion is what the individual does with his own solitariness.*

Philosopher **John Dewey** (1859-1952) defined religion as *the active relationship between the ideal and the actual.*

The famous theologian **Paul Tillich** (1886-1965) described the human propensity toward religion as *being grasped by an ultimate concern, a concern which qualifies all other concerns as preliminary and which itself contains the answer to the question of a meaning of our life.*

Harvard Philosopher **William Ernest Hocking** (1873-1966) in *The Meaning of God in Human Experience: A Philosophic Study of*

Religion suggests: *religion lies close to the primitive moving-forces of life: deeper then, than reason or any work of reason.*

Anthropologist **Clifford Geertz** (1926-2006) in his 1963 work entitled *The Interpretation of Cultures* wrote that: *Religion is a system of symbols which acts to establish powerful, pervasive, and long-lasting moods and motivations in men by formulating conceptions of a general order of existence, clothing these conceptions which such an aura of factuality that the moods and motivations seem uniquely realistic.*

David V. Barrett in his 2001 work, *The New Believers: Sects Cults and Alternative Religions*, says religion is: *a social construct encompassing beliefs and practices which enable people, individually and collectively, to make some sense of the great questions of life and death.*

The renowned religion scholar **Jonathan Z. Smith** wrote: *one may clarify the term religion by defining it as a system of beliefs and practices that are relative to superhuman beings. This definition* *moves away from defining religion as some special kind of experience or worldview. It emphasizes that religions are systems or structures consisting of specific kinds of beliefs and practices: beliefs and practices that are related to superhuman beings. Superhuman beings are beings that can do things ordinary mortals cannot do. They are known for their miraculous deeds and powers that set them apart from humans. They can either be male or female, or androgynous. They need not be gods or goddesses, but may take the form of an ancestor that affects our lives. They may take the form of malevolent or benevolent spirits who cause good or harm to a person or community. Furthermore, the definition requires that such superhuman beings be specifically related to beliefs and practices, myths, and rituals.*

Ninian Smart (1927-2001) developed a more encompassing model of the phenomenological approach to religion, which also made room for a more sensible inclusion of the Eastern traditions. He suggested that the sacred makes itself known in any number of seven different avenues or showings. Smart includes: 1) the doctrinal and philosophical, (2) the mythical, (3) the ethical, (4) the experiential, (5) ritual, (6) social, and (7) material. Smart's understanding of religious tradition is that each group possesses a core of beliefs, a narrative that explains and justifies them, an ethical framework or code that guides adherents through life, an emotional component and request for commitment that ties believers to the movement, a set of rituals, routines or practices that keep them on track, and an institutional structure, or physical structures, as well as a culture or community that enables them to act and live out their beliefs and undertakings within.

4

What are the Differences Between the Disciplines of Philosophy, Theology, and Religion?

Quite as few years ago I did some teaching at The Ohio State University. Their religion courses were housed in the Department of Comparative Studies. The idea for keeping religion safely in that interdisciplinary setting dates back to a movement during the late 1960's and early 1970's in the United States when secular institutions of higher learning began to create opportunities to engage in the study of religion at non-denominational settings. I was thankful for the opportunity to work at a large secular university but had received much of my graduate and undergraduate training at small denominational colleges and universities, studying in the general areas of Theology and Philosophy. Soon after arriving at OSU, I can clearly recall (mainly because it was a source of some embarrassment) having a conversation with religion professor Lindsay Jones who was a former student of the famous religion scholar Mircea Eliade. Dr. Jones had just been asked to take on the role of editor-in-chief for an updating of the acclaimed *Encyclopedia of Religion* (published by the University of Chicago), a work that his mentor, Eliade, had previously supervised. Jones mentioned to me that he was hoping to be able to include a few new articles and updates by Jonathan Smith, who he personally knew. Being a medievalist, I asked, "how do you know Jonathan Riley-Smith" (the famous Crusade historian from Great Britain)? Jones replied, "not Riley-Smith, Jonathan Z. Smith". Having focused on Monastic Studies and Divinity for much of my graduate work, I felt some regret in saying I was not aware of the work of Jonathan Z. Smith, who is a significant University of Chicago religion scholar. That was probably because up until that point in my career I had only taken a few odd courses in departments of Religious Studies, mainly as a transient student. Just a few years before my time at Ohio State, Smith had written an article entitled "Are Theological and Religious Studies Compatible?" While there is much overlap between the Study of Religion and the field of Theology, I have become increasingly aware throughout my career that there are many differences. Jonathan Z. Smith had spent a portion of his academic life (almost to the point of weariness, as he notes) fleshing out these very issues. He writes: "From the perspective of the academic study of religion, theology is datum, the theologian is a native informant".[1] Smith also directs our attention to the work of fellow religion scholar Eric J. Sharpe (1933-2000) who believes that Theology "attempts to affirm…some dominant religious tradition" and "attempts to look beyond traditions to some ultimate reality…beyond religious phenomena to their ultimate significance".[2] One of the big differences seems to be experiential. Those in the field of Religious Studies are examining information about cultures and movements. Those in Theology are looking to explain an actual relationship that they believe to exist between humanity and the divine. In the study of religion, scholars examine perceived relationships. Smith also points out that academic Religious Studies have "muscled-in on the turf" that was previously dominated by Theology. To put it succinctly: not all Religion is Philosophy, not all Theology is Philosophy, some Philosophy spills into Religion, and all of Theology can be objectively examined in The Study of Religion (even the miraculous, because it is studied, just not necessarily believed).

In some contemporary contexts, a distinction is made between theology (which is seen as involving some level of commitment to the claims of the religious tradition being studied), and religious studies (which is normally seen as requiring that the question of the truth or falsehood of the religious traditions studied is kept apart from the investigation.) Theological Study, due to its historical connections to monotheism and the study of Christianity is not a methodology that is necessarily easy to transfer to other religious traditions. It is not a neutral perspective. Religious

Studies involves the investigation of historical or contemporary practices, communities, or ideas. Scholars use intellectual tools and

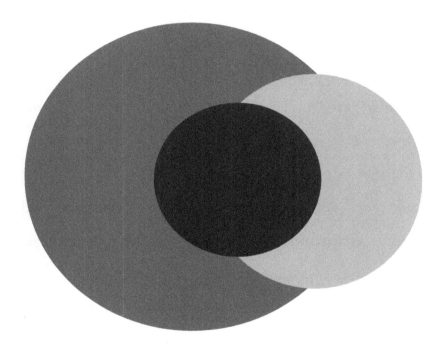

frameworks that are not themselves specifically tied to any religious tradition, using approaches that are normally understood to be neutral or secular. In contexts where Religious Studies in this sense is the focus, the primary forms of study are likely to include: Anthropology of Religion, Comparative Religion, History of Religions, Philosophy of Religion, Psychology of Religion, Sociology of Religion. But Jonathan Z. Smith points out that the potential breadth and scope is not limited:

Religion is solely the creation of the scholar's study. It is created for the scholar's analytic purposes by his imaginative acts of comparison and generalization. Religion has no independent existence apart from the academy. For this reason, the student of religion, and most particularly the historian of religion, must be relentlessly self-conscious. Indeed, this self-consciousness constitutes his primary expertise, his foremost object of study.[3]

As we have noted, Theology and Religious Studies are regarded by some scholars to be in tension, but they are often held to coexist, without serious tension. It is sometimes denied that there is even a clear or absolute boundary between them. Sheila Greeve Davaney in her chapter on "Rethinking Theology and Religious Studies" writes:

*To put it bluntly, religious studies have increasingly become inhospitable toward theology. For many tellers of this tale, the best **symbol** for these developments is the Dutch Universities Act of 1876, whereby the sciences of religion now became a field of study within Dutch state universities and [the] dogmatic and practical theology were remanded to denominational seminaries.*[4]

In the United States today, The Study of Religion includes studying Theology, but Theology departments themselves are found mostly in seminaries and denominational colleges, which are more focused on training pastors and preserving religious traditions. There are some exceptions (University of Virginia, Arizona State, University of Kansas, University of Southern Mississippi, to name a few). Some of this had to do with earlier misguided notions of the separation of Church and State as well as legislation that occurred in the 1950's and 60's in regard to religious expressions and viewpoints at public educational institutions. Certain determinations historically were made by individual states. The Study of Religion was for the most part absent in public institutions for fear that teaching "about" religion might be construed as the teaching "of" religion.[5] However, in the past 40 years this has all changed (certainly much more since I started teaching religion at the college level some 30 years ago). But, as I previously mentioned, Religious Studies in secular universities are often housed in broader departments like Humanities or Comparative Studies.

Philosophy

How about Philosophy? If we accept Anselm of Canterbury's (1033-1109) definition of theology as "faith seeking understanding", the theologian is a believer within a system seeking to identify the core beliefs, their meanings, and implications. In Philosophy of Religion, the personal belief system of the scholar is theoretically irrelevant to the enterprise. (It may be irrelevant but I find it hard to think we can keep our disposition of belief completely out of our minds or the discussion.) Theology in most cases presupposes divine revelation. Philosophy does not. Philosophy assumes the role of critic of all major human practices, including the practice of Religion. The reflections of Theology are generated from a place of faith or religious conviction and believe we are answerable to a source or force that initiates human existence. For Western Scholars (Jewish, Christian and Muslim), beginning in the early Middle Ages, philosophical discourse served as a form of apologetics for the theologian.[5] For a time, using reason, the two disciplines were almost joined. But, as we have mentioned in previous chapters, by the time we get to the Enlightenment period of the 18th century, there is a growing separation between the disciplines of Philosophy and Theology which is based mostly on metaphysical principles (dealing with first principles, some of them abstract, including knowing, being, cause, effect, time, possibility), and empirical (observable and verifiable) understanding. Philosophy begins to ally itself with the natural sciences while theology attempted to reconcile revealed scriptures and doctrines with an evolving modern worldview. In the Eastern world, things are seen a bit differently, as philosophies and religion have traditionally not been as separated as they now seem to be in the West. Impermanence, as expressed in Buddhist and Hindu traditions left open the door to uncertainty. Eastern philosophies seem to reflect the idea that things are conditioned by our thoughts.[6] Philosophical notions of interconnectedness and harmony present in Eastern philosophies have served to soften debates between religious and philosophical reason or empirical understandings. However, we need to note that knowing with absolute certainty about literal religious teachings, like the role of the gods, or revelatory nature of the Eastern scriptures have radically been questioned as far back as the time of Confucius, Buddha, Lao Tzu and Mahavira in the 6th century BCE. So there can be a sharp divide between a number of religious teachings, folk religion, and the philosophies in the Eastern world.

In the West the separation and criticism between philosophy and theology did not get aggressive until the late 1700's. It is around this time that distinctions began to be made about the sub-field of the Philosophy of Religion. Philosophers of Religion, like Linda Zagzebski, say Philosophy of Religion is part of Philosophy, not Religion. Much of what is done today in the Philosophy of Religion was once part of traditional Philosophy. The Philosophy of Religion employs Logic. Logic is a branch of philosophy concerned with the distinction between correct and incorrect reasoning. It commonly comprises both deductive (conclusions based on general principles or premises) and inductive (moving from specific information to a conclusion) arguments. It is possible to distinguish correct reasoning from incorrect reasoning. Logic is the discipline that studies this distinction. It helps us control the conditions under which the truth of certain beliefs can lead us to a correct understanding. Logic also draws attention to ways we may be led to believe something when it is not true. Now logic cannot completely guarantee we will always arrive at the truth. Often the perspectives and beliefs that we begin with can be in error. However, by following the principles of correct reasoning, we may be able to keep additional missteps in reason from leaking into our study.

As mentioned in our first chapter, the evolution of modern philosophy had much to do with the development of critical approaches to the issue of faith and practice of religion. Many saw faith and religious activity as illogical. The German philosopher Immanuel Kant (1724-1804) articulates his strongest criticisms against religious organizations and practices seeing religion as a "counterfeit service to God". Among the major targets of his criticism are: external ritual, superstition and a hierarchical church order. He sees all of these as efforts to make oneself pleasing to God. Kant launched severe criticisms on these matters, along with his rejection of the possibility of theoretical proofs for the existence of God. While Kant's idea of God evolves throughout his life and work he later comes to a notion of God as "an ideal of human reason". He identifies God with our concept of the highest moral duty rather than as an independent substance. Kant then comes to the notion of an immanent God (that is, one internal to our world rather than transcendently separate from it). While this line of thinking was not fully resolved by Kant himself, it would be developed later by German Idealists (most significantly, Hegel). Rather than still postulating God as an independent reality, Kant says that "God and the world are correlates," interdependent and mutually implicating one another. Kant put forth the notion God is in us, rather than seeing us in God. He indicated that, although God is different from us, God exists in an ideal rather than substantial from. He also philosophically re-interprets some basic Christian doctrines, seeing Jesus Christ as the affirmation of a "pure moral disposition of the heart" that "can make man well-pleasing to God". Regarding Kant's conception of religion, some critics have pointed to his *Deism* (belief in a God who set the world into motion and let it then operate on the principles of nature and science). In 1793, Kant wrote a book entitled *Religion within the Boundaries of Bare Reason.* In it we see Kant rationally reducing religiosity, turning religion toward morality, and seeing Christianity to be primarily about ethics.

Also, instrumental in articulating the divide between theology and philosophy was David Hume (1711-1776), a Scottish thinker who was known for developing a fairly radical *empirical* (based upon observation and physical evidence) philosophical system. Hume was also a naturalist, and highly skeptical of traditional religious doctrines and dogmas. In his work, *A Treatise of Human Nature* (1739), he attempted to work toward a more naturalistic science of humanity, looking at the psychological basis for what drives our nature. During Hume's time, there was a philosophical debate raging between the "religious philosophers" and "speculative atheists". Hume sided with ideas put forth by British philosopher Thomas Hobbes (1588-1679) that were based upon empiricist principles. Hume believed that we might need to be skeptical about the human foundations of our knowledge of God. Hobbes had likened our knowledge of God to a blind man's perception of fire. Proceeding from a finite human position, how could we fully know about the infinite, if that is in fact what we believe God to be? Hume believed polytheism to be the original starting point of belief for humanity. He said people moved toward monotheism more out of passion than reason, not out of logic, but out of fear. As his contemporaries moved further away from an anthropomorphic God, Hume believed in the necessity of religious leaders and scholars to interpret and mediate the invisible. This attack was aimed in particular at the Catholic Church, its institutions, and its teaching. He was particularly bothered by the metaphysical absurdity of the doctrine of *Real Presence* (the Roman Catholic literal notion of Christ's presence in the bread and wine transformed at the liturgy). However, he also rejected the truths of revealed religions (not only miracles, but the process of revelation itself), which formed the very basis for the Protestant worldview of his day.

Against the philosophical *rationalists* (articulating reality through reason), Hume held that passion rather than reason governs human behavior. He argued against the existence of innate ideas (pre-existing in our minds, as thought by Socrates and Plato). The position of innate ideas was used by medieval thinkers to help prove existence of God, suggesting that if all ideas were real, and already existing in our minds, then the idea of God must be real and God must exist in reality because he put the idea of himself in us. Hume disagreed, supporting the claim of Aristotle that all human knowledge is ultimately found in our experience. He saw the mind as a "bundle of perceptions", the self as a bundle of experiences linked by cause and memory.

Hume wrote substantially against belief in miracles. He believed the world was governed by the laws of nature that are matters of fact, they are universal, and exhibit no contradiction. He once said that while we might enjoy the story of a miracle, it is in reality a violation of nature. Hume went on to argue that miracles in rival religions might serve to discredit one another. He suggested that no matter how convincing an account or witness of a miracle was, it can never approach the weight of the unwavering laws of nature. For Hume, the cause of a miracle is believed to be something outside nature. Measuring one's belief against physical evidence, a wise man must reject the fantastic.

During the Enlightenment, there was a tension between two major poles of traditional Christian belief: *revealed religion* and *natural religion*. Revealed religion encompasses the avenues of experience, contact, or knowledge of God through an encounter or the reading of revealed texts contained in the Bible, including prophesies, voices, and miracles. These revelations are direct interventions of the deity in earthly affairs. *Natural religion* intimates a knowledge of God that comes from our experiences in the everyday scientifically oriented world using reason and logic to understand the things around us. *Natural Religion* relies on logical understandings of our existence including perception of God through causality, design, and our observable functioning of the natural world in relation to its creator. In his various treatises, Hume attacks both natural and revealed religion.

Despite Hume's skepticism about religious belief, it is likely that he was not a complete atheist. Some suggest he favored a type of Deism that might link to his belief in causality. However, he likely believed there was never enough evidence to support or justify any religious position. While he did not subscribe to traditional theological viewpoints, he never completely ruled out the reality of "ideas" about a God. But it would not be until we get to Ludwig Feuerbach (1804-1872) that God would be treated solely as an idea. Hume's influence extended to the 19th century existentialist Kierkegaard (1813-1855), who would follow up on moving beyond the "idea" of God, more importantly drawing upon Hume's arguments against rational theology. For Kierkegaard, faith had to be a leap. Hume also influenced an important early religion scholar, William James (1842-1910), especially in his work the "Will to Believe". The 20th century philosopher Ludwig Wittgenstein (1889-1951), who attempted to re-open the door to the possibility of religious connections, built his work upon Hume's scholarship. Wittgenstein suggested that logic and empirical evidence were ways of understanding that were quite different from the language one might possibly use to express religion. While he said it was always hard for him to "bend the knee" he believed a religious approach to life was important. Wittgenstein spent a good deal of time wrestling with the issues of language and religion. Kierkegaard, James, and Wittgenstein all happen fall into the *epistemological* (study of truth) category of *Fideism,* the belief that reason cannot bring one to faith.[7] This journey to the question of belief brings us back full circle to The Study of Religion which examines and appreciates all these positions discussed in this chapter: the rational, ritualistic, emotional, relational, agnostic, atheistic and experiential.

1. Jonathan Z. Smith, "Are Theological and Religious Studies Compatible?", reprinted in Chapter 7, *On Teaching Religion*, Oxford University Press (2013).

2. Eric J. Sharpe, "The Compatibility of Theological and Religious Studies: Historical Theoretical and Contemporary Perspectives", *Bulletin of the Council of Societies for the Study of Religion* 26, no.3 (1997).

3. Jonathan Z. Smith, *Imagining Religion: From Babylon to Jonestown* (Chicago: University of Chicago Press, 1982), xi

4. Sheila Greeve Davaney, "Rethinking Theology and Religious Studies", Chapter 10, *Religious Studies, Theology and University*, State University of New York Press (2002), p.140.

5. John J. McGonagle Jr., "Teaching About Religion in The Public College and University: A Legal and Educational Analysis", *The American University Law Review*, Vol 20 (1970)

6. Hilary Rodrigues and John S. Harding, *Introduction to the Study of Religion*, Routledge (2001), p. 26.

7. *Ibid.*, p. 29.

8. Linda Zagzebski, *The Philosophy of Religion: An Historical Introduction*, Blackwell *(2007)*.

5

From the Phenomenological to the

Void

Personal Insights into the Nature of Religion and its Study

While Religion, History, Sociology, Literature, Psychology and Science and Philosophy are seen as distinct fields, in my professional practice I have come to appreciate how they can often be joined in interdisciplinary fashion. Continuing to immerse oneself in a breadth of historical and religious topics allows the bias of disciplines, theories, and methodologies to soften and causes perceptions of delineation and traditional divisions to move one toward a broader range of perception. Throughout my own education and in the process of educating college students from a variety of disciplines I have found that critical thinking, a sense of history, along with an openness and tolerance for many voices and opinions is what needs to be the true basis for any sort of liberal education. I also believe this is the key to approaching ideological religious questions for which no single individual, group or discipline have been able to perfectly answer.

Throughout time, groups routinely seem to have been able to sets standards by which they can determine ideas or beliefs to be right or wrong. Yet, contradictory or prevailing opinion does not always stop those who have embraced an ideology that gives new meaning to their lives. This may be the reason we have so many religions. Humanity has long been socialized into systems that teach that the opinions, beliefs, laws and interpretations of morality by some "authority" (be it divine or human) matter very much. But there are always those who appear to be driven away by such dogged perceptions of truth and moved toward modified (if not at times contrary) causes, practices and lifestyles. The interesting part that history plays in all this (while it seeks to systematize and integrate information) is that such accounts can often result in a further contortion of reality. The manner in which religious phenomena, experience, philosophy and scholarship are interpreted, depicted and presented to subsequent observers could be affected by the agenda (conscious or unconscious) of the chronicler. The methodology for historical portrayal is in itself an art and the results are often quite subjective.

One of the things I chosen to examine in my doctoral studies was how groups as well as individuals have been able to work out their sense of ultimate reality. In the face of all that has come before us we seem to be constantly re-balancing our human needs in a way that will provide us with the greatest attainable good. How does one's sense of ultimate reality relate to tradition, knowledge, the needs of present generations, as well as any possible projections for the future? How can we responsibly re-tell stories (particularly those of religious communities) in a way that does justice to those cultures that have come before us while making their ideas understandable to those who will hear, read about, and experience remnants of their history today?

For most of my professional life (over the past thirty years) I have concerned myself with the study of religion from a variety of perspectives. My current interests pertain to the development of historical, sociological, theological and cultural understandings of world religions, both present and past. Involvement with various curriculums at different universities has led me to teach over 530 sections of twenty four different college courses ranging from Comparative Religious Studies to courses on Eastern Religion, The Christian Tradition, Hebrew Bible, Religion in America, Philosophy of Religion, New Testament Studies, Ethics, Native American Religion, Integrative and Intercultural Studies, Introductions to Philosophy, Courses on Human Nature, Ancient and Medieval Civilizations, Contemporary History, Social Justice, and Theological Problems. The approaches I have chosen in directing these studies involves a good deal of interdisciplinary and intercultural investigation.

One of the things I have discovered through various interactions with college learners of all ages is that other cultures and ideas are most comfortably understood in light of our own. While comparisons can never be identical, there are basic philosophies, practices and ideals that transcend specific cultures, religions and ideologies. After we have unpacked our own baggage and are surprised by things we have found it is often easier to embrace the unexpected in other systems. But only by attempting to "unfold" our own we actually begin to understand the levels of culture, superstition, philosophy and deep piety that other religions have to offer. If one is to truly appreciate American religion, including its roots and possibilities for the future, we must first have a basic understanding of world religions, both historic and present. As educational leaders and learners, if we can at least begin to openly appreciate that all religious and philosophical systems are, or at one time were (that is meaningful movements toward ultimate reality however anyone chooses to define them), then we are on our way to a more open comparative study. In an academic environment, this is the posture with which we should strive to approach all human ideas, no matter how much we might personally disagree with their ideology or the outcome of their implementation.

Phenomenological Aspects of Religion

We ended the last chapter with the notion of the leap of faith. For those who still believed, scholars in the 19th and 20th centuries were looking for some sort of measurement in order to know if the object of people's worship or ritual expression was real. Scientologists even came up the e-meter to gauge responses for those on their way to clarity. One of the ways to better understand and categorize (both for today and in the past) the religious encounters people believe they have had is to look toward applying a phenomenological approach to the study of people's experiences. Phenomena are objects of a person's perception, either through the senses or the mind, which they believe to be real. The mode of study is not limited to one area of social science like psychology. It also included anthropology, sociology as well as hard physical science. It can be done by those who are part of a particular tradition, or those outside it. There were even those involved with the study of religion that tried to detect a larger phenomenological pattern, the essence of a common experience for those encountering the divine or a sacred presence. Was there something to a religious experience in general that people might agree upon and share? Rudolf Otto (1869-1937) was a German Lutheran theologian and philosopher who became one of the important and influential voices in early twentieth-century who embarked upon such a study. Although a trained theologian, Otto began to use the principles of religious studies to make larger claims about the religious experience. In his work, *The Idea of the Holy*, he introduces the concept of the *numinous*, which he believed was at the center of human religiosity throughout the world. Otto saw the encounter that humanity had with the *numinous* as both non-rational and non-sensory. It was a "feeling" that was outside of the self. He also believed the experience of the holy could manifest itself in two types of expressions which he terms *mysterium tremendum*, the mystery that terrifies, and *mysterium fascinocium* (or "mysterium fascinans"), the mystery that attracts.[1]

Naming and Experiencing the Ineffable

Most religions attempt to identify, understand, and experience the ultimate reality they believe holds and controls all of life and the universe. Some are content to know that they can never know or fully understand for sure. Others freely admit to both knowing and experiencing. Phenomenologists of religion study the experiential elements and try to conceptualize them. Early proponents of this approach were William B. Kristensen (1867-1953) and Gerardus van der Leeuw (1890-1950). Kristensen was looking for the meaning that religious phenomena might have to those who claim to experience it. Writings and speech of the believers were a good place to start. Some of this work had to be quite specific to particular groups and individuals. Both Kristensen and van der Leeuw included Rudolf Otto's understanding of the Holy (marked by awe or fear) when it came to the awareness of the unfolding of sacred experiences. Gerardus van der Leeuw wrote about the different ways that the sacred was perceived (direct experience, understanding, expression) through 3 levels of sacred appearance, which he described as: concealment (*Verborgenheit*), transparency (*Durchsichtigkeit*), and evelation (*Offenbarwerden*). He went on to suggest that:

> *... phenomenologists of religion seek to suspend their beliefs about religions in order to describe them in their own terms from a standpoint that is "empathetic" with their respective adherents. Phenomenology of religion is also comparative, seeking out aspects of religious life that are, its proponents suggest, universal or essential rather than applicable only to particular traditions.*[2]

Mircea Eliade (1907-1986), a Romanian philosopher and professor of religion made significant strides toward a contemporary understanding of how humans in general experience the phenomena of the divine but went well beyond the work of his predecessors. He spent a number of his formative years in India studying philosophy and religion. Eliade came to the United States in 1956 after two decades of political involvements in Europe, and spent much of the remainder of his esteemed career at the University of Chicago. His important work, *The Sacred and the Profane,* pointed out how myth, ritual, religious observance, and awareness of mystery, both through time and in the present brought people to an understanding of things elevated to a heightened experience. He suggested that the divine breaks into the human experience in some tangible recognizable form. Such an in-breaking is known as a *hierophany*.[3] These manifestations become the touchstones by which humanity identifies their relationship with the divine or ultimate reality. This experience of the sacred might constitute the inception of devotions that form the trappings of religious traditions. Eliade and Otto both saw the sacred as *transhistorical* (beyond the boundaries of history and occurring throughout human history), *existential* (experienced in the here and now), but also unaffected by the flow of societal changes. Not attempting to focus on any specific historical context allowed Eliade see how a variety of ideas, patterns, in-breakings, and manifestations of the sacred could be similar across time and space. [4] Critics of the phenomenological approach might question the universal applications of Eliade, Otto, and van der Leeuw, accusing them of an approach that might work well for Europeans and other western religions, especially those that have a God, but in reality might not apply so well to certain Buddhist or Confucian traditions.

Religious questions of origin and order first came from the human need to ground our understanding of the universe in something beyond scientific facts and hypotheses. The phenomenological approach to religion on some level renewed the quest for an experience of this reality in the modern age. Langdon

Gilkey (1919-2004) continued some of the work of Rudlof Otto and Mircea Eliade by trying to articulate the *numinous, holy,* or *sacred* in his books *Naming the Whirlwind: The Renewal of God-Language* and in his subsequent *Reaping the Whirlwind.* For Gilkey, God becomes the name of the principle that ties together the mysteries of the universe and symbolically grounds the notion of Ultimate Reality. Religion attempts to know it and endeavors to experience what constitutes that reality (if in fact it is at all a reality, or a symbol for human need). Gilkey wrote:

> *...our experiences of the sacred always come to us, as we have shown, in connection of our awareness of the finite... The sacred, the numinous, what we have called the category of the ultimate, has appeared everywhere in human life an in connection with all sorts of experiences. But when men become aware of it, it has never felt like an ordinary experience, as if it were merely a part of the ordinary sequence of natural or historical events. In all of religion, the sacred, while in and through the profane [the ordinary], has not been experienced as a part or even an inference from*

the profane; and accordingly, experience of it had been demarked as a special kind of experience."[5]

Revelation

Divine revelation is one of the major sources of impetus for a majority of world religions and denominations. This was certainly true historically and continues to be embraced by many religious adherents today. Harvard Philosopher William Ernest Hocking (1873-1966) wrote:

There is no religion without a basis in revelation, and therefore it must be possible for such religion to be re-conceptualized in the light of the revelatory ingredients in the others.[6]

Agreement on what divine revelation actually is, and what constitutes it, has been a source of disagreement among historical religions, their successors, and modern counterparts. Many believe divine revelation to be absolutely real, others are cautious about its reception, while some feel it is completely imagined. Most monotheistic traditions (including Zoroastrianism), as well as Hinduism, believe their sacred scriptures are divinely inspired revelations. Countless believers would hold that any in-breaking or inspiration of the divine constitutes a form of revelation. For many adherents, the scriptures are believed to be the direct word of God, or the gods, delivered by prophets, teachers, writers, angels, messengers, or the Holy Spirit. Interpreters of the Christian Gospels even claim certain sections contain the *ipsissima verba*, the actual words of Christ himself. Absolutely rigid adherence to principles of revelation is the underlying root of Fundamentalism, which we examined in a previous section. Within the Christian tradition a number of critical European scholars began addressing the notion of scriptural interpretation and strict adherence to revelation during the 1800's. The Historical-Critical Method (which we examined in a previous section) was born from these endeavors. The literary devices of myth and metaphor have been used to explain certain inconsistencies or impossibilities that exist in the sacred scriptures. Some adherents fully believe their scriptures are revealed, other suggest they are inspired faith documents, while other claims only certain passages are the word of God (or gods). The question of which parts of the scriptures might come directly from divine sources is a hotly contested issue. In my opinion, among the revealed religions, the notion of revelation is one of the major interpretive problems as well as source of divisions facing religious groups today. Translations of scriptures into contemporary languages are also an issue that contemporary Historical-Critical scholars have continued to deal with. Research and dialogue are ongoing. There are also religious groups, the Roman Catholic Church is one example,[7] that believe divine revelation extends outside the scriptures through Sacred Tradition and interpretation by the teaching authority within the group. Many Christian denominations see divine revelation extending to ordinary individuals through the Holy Spirit. Outside the scriptures, Latter-Day Saints,[8] Bahai Faith, some Pentecostal groups, and certain Quakers and a few modern Taoist groups believe in the notion of Continuous Revelation, and within Islam there are certain groups that leave themselves open to the possibility.

Questioning Religious Authority and Traditional Views of God

The questioning of religious institutions has been present, right from the very beginning and throughout the history religious activity. In times of societal crisis even particular gods were called into question. The beauty of ancient polytheism was that if the prayers and offering you were making to a particular god were not working, there were always many more gods to which you could appeal. Monotheism gradually changed our options, at least in regard to the issue of questioning gods and appealing to new ones. It may actually have taken a few devastating conquests of the Chosen People (ancient Jews) for them to adjust to the new monotheistic worldview. While certain religious institutions and authorities were called to question during the middle ages, in the early modern world, the Protestant Reformation and the radical phase of the French Revolution (between 1792-1794) sought to remedy problems of religious institutional authority. The Church no longer spoke for God. For a time, at least in Protestant circles, the Bible became the source of authority, but shortly thereafter that was called into question with the historical-critical method. With regard to the contemporary study of religion, there were several pivotal ideologues that helped change the conversation and paradigm of how modern scholars began to think of the divine.

Fredrich Nietzsche (1844-1900), in his work *The Gay Science,* re-visits the idea of The Death of God upon a modern readership. In Nietzsche's parable, a man is running through the streets frantically searching for God, but not able to find him. Nonbelievers stand by and make fun of him. In frustration, the man shouts aloud:

Where has God gone? ... I shall tell you. We have killed him – you and I. We are his murderers... Do you not hear anything yet of the noise of the gravediggers who are

> *burying God? Do we not smell anything yet of God's decomposition? Gods too decompose. God is Dead. God remains dead. And we have killed him. How shall we murder of all murders console ourselves? That which was the holiest and mightiest of all that the world yet possessed has bled to death under our knives... With what water could we purify ourselves? What festivals of atonement, what sacred games shall we need to invent ... Must we not ourselves become gods simply to be worthy of it?"* ... *on the same day, the madman entered diverse churches and there sang a requiem... "what are these churches now if they are not the tombs and sepulchers of* God?"[9]

Neitzsche may not have literally believed there was no God, but as an existentialist philosopher he was not able to actually apprehend the real presence of God in modern times. He was not the first thinker to bring up the concept. Philosopher Georg Hegel (1770-1831), in his *Phenomenology of Spirit* wrote:

> *...the feeling that God Himself is dead, the feeling which was uttered by Pascal... purely as a phase, but also as no more than just a phase, of the highest idea.*[10]

Traditional notions of God were dying off in favor of the evolving concepts in the scientific world. If God were still to be seen as the absolute giver of revelation for humanity, in an educated world, rational options for an understanding of revelation were becoming limited. The notions that the Judeo-Christian God was beginning to be radically questioned, or the possibility of God becoming somehow irrelevant to the function of society, had now begun to creep into the consciousness of Europeans. However, Nietzsche did believe there was hope for humanity without clinging to the traditional concept of God. Giving up belief in a somewhat misguided path opened the way toward more creative human possibilities, finding answers in this world, not the supernatural. Traditional religion would no longer impede the progress of humanity.

Taking this a step further, some 50 years later, another German scholar who was an activist and pastor, Dietrich Bonhoeffer, became critical of traditional forms of religion and the leadership of society. He suggested that the superficial nature of religion belied the true essence of Christianity. Like Luther, Bonhoeffer spoke out against the "cheap grace" of the Church that was "sold on the marketplace" and began to suggest God had taken a giant step backward. There was a huge gap in our understanding of God that needed to be filled with the modern embrace of theories of evolution and advancements in psychology. In a plea for a religion-less Christianity he wrote: "God as a working hypothesis in morals, politics or science has been surmounted and abolished, and the same thing has happened in philosophy and religion".[11] Bonhoeffer had problems with the separation between the sacred and the secular that had occurred and wished to return to a secular suffering example of Christ as a starting point for religious discussion. He never believed there was no God, but said that Christians need to cease to be religious. In 1936 Bonhoeffer was ousted from his teaching position at the University of Berlin, went on to conduct an underground seminary, taught in the United States in 1939, but returned to Germany to re-engage in critical teaching and ministry. In 1943 he imprisoned by the Nazis and later executed.

Religion in the Secular City

In 1979, while I was a student at St. Paul Seminary in Ottawa Canada, I encountered a book by Peter Berger entitled *A Rumor of Angels*. It appeared on the supplemental reading list for my course in Fundamental Theology. Berger's book was of course not about angels but about how the secularization of society had relegated our view of the "transcendent" to a place of mere "rumor".[12] Outside of its contents, one of the reasons the book was so memorable is that title alone had spurred an opportunity for debate about angels in one of our classroom sessions. That same week we were visited by our bishop of the Diocese of Burlington Vermont, John Marshall. He took the time to personally visit with each of us (I think we had a total 4 seminarians from Vermont that year) and I quite vividly recall a very uncomfortable conversation that I had with him in my dorm room. The bishop asked about what I was learning and how I was enjoying my time in Canada. Eager to impress him (and quite oblivious to the fact that he was one of the most conservative bishops in the entire United States) I began to relay the details of the rather exciting discussion we had about angles in our Theology class. I told him that I had often considered the possibility that angels were not real. Maybe they were just metaphors for perceived divine inspirations. Within the year, Marshall, who (unbeknownst to me had been appointed by the Vatican to investigate student life and curriculum at the major North American Seminaries) began to systematically withdraw us all from the most liberal graduate schools and began a crackdown of the more forward thinking Roman Catholic academic programs, which affectionately (or infamously) became known as The Marshall Plan.

Over a decade before my own seminary experience, following the lead of Vatican II in the 1960's Catholic Church, and with the radical changes in Protestant theological views, an Andover Newton School of Theology professor named Harvey

Cox published an important book called *The Secular City*. Its thesis was that traditional religion in the modern world was collapsing amid the rise of secular urban culture. Autonomy, mobility, convenience, and widespread educational opportunities, which were emerging within a framework of technological and scientific advancements, were causing the disruption of organized religion and traditional religious worldviews. Cox described the effects of this secularization as "the loosing of the world from religion...the breaking of all supernatural myths and sacred symbols".[13] The secularized world was interested in the here and now, not some realm or god beyond it. Society had begun to lose trust in religious morality, rituals and rules. Large numbers of people stopped going to church, or were leaving their churches for alternative practices. A similar exodus had long been going on for a decade or so in Europe.

Death of God Movement

The 1960's saw an increased protest of organized religion but also brought back some of the philosophical underpinnings of Bonhoeffer and Nietzsche under the guise of an ideology that defined itself as Christian Atheism. Theology professors William Hamilton and Thomas Altizer popularized the Death-of-God movement. Joined by scholars such as Gabriel Vahanian (who actually wrote a book called *The Death of God*), a call for an end to the culture of Christianity and outmoded religiosity was extended. Hamilton took an even more staunchly atheist position than his predecessors when he wrote:

> *there once was a God to which adoration, praise and trust were appropriate, possible, and even necessary, but there is now no such God... If there was a God and there now isn't, it should be possible to indicate why this change took place, when it took place, and who was responsible for it... We are not talking about the absence of the experience of God, but about the experience of the absence of God... the 19th century made it real and today it is our turn to understand and accept it."*[14]

The movement expressed that it was time for humanity to stop hiding behind some hope in the transcendent and begin bearing responsibility in the here and now through both suffering and love. While suffering and love are the symbols of Christ, they are the reality of humanity. Now that God had withdrawn from the world it was time for humanity to squarely face life and death on their own terms. The philosopher Michel Foucault (1926-1984) once wrote of the new age of academic theological investigation:

The central question here is whether man is a figure that is in some ways correlative with God. Man might have metaphorically killed God as an all-knowing metaphysical entity, a source of all values and eternal ideas, but he does little to question the primacy of the space that God has occupied. Whether or not God is real, we cannot seem to stop referencing Him, situating his language, his thought, his laughter at the center of the post-Enlightenment world.[15]

1. Rudolf Otto, *The Idea of the Holy*

2. Gerardus van der Leeuw, *Religion in Essence and Manifestation: A Study in Phenomenology*, (1933).

3. Mircea Eliade, *The Sacred and the Profane*

4. Hilary Rodrigues and John Harding, *Introduction to the Study of Religion*, Routledge (2009), p. 79.

5. Gilkey, *Naming the Whirlwind* p. 441-5

6. William Ernest Hocking, *Living Religions in a World of Faith*

7. See *Dei Verbum* in The Documents of Vatican II (1965) on the Catholic position regarding divine revelation.

8. There is a good article entitled "Divine Revelation in Modern Times" on the Church of Jesus Christ of Latter-Day Saints *Newsroom* website (12 December, 2011) http://www.mormonnewsroom.org/article/divine-revelation-modern-times

9. Friedrich Nietzsche, *The Gay Science* (1882)

10. Georg Hegel, *The Phenomenology of Spirit* (1845)

11. Dietrich Bonhoeffer, *Letters and Papers from Prison*, (1965).

12. Peter Berger, *A Rumor of Angels: Modern Society and the Rediscovery of the Supernatural,* Anchor Books (1970).

13. Harvey Cox, *The Secular City* (1965), p.1.

14. "The Death of God" in *Playboy* (13) August 1966

15. Michel Foucault, *The Archaeology of Knowledge & The Discourse on Language,* Pantheon (1972)

6

Questions and Perspectives for Contemporary Religion

Why (and how) Do We Believe?

Often on the first day of class in my Comparative Religion course I do an exercise with students where I have them list reasons for believing in God, a Higher Power, or source of Ultimate Reality. Without the benefit of any previous methodological and philosophical orientation in the study of religion (but sometimes with a bit of prompting) they are usually able to pinpoint the major reasons for belief that are historically identified by the scholarly community in the field of Religious Studies. As we have previously mentioned, sociologists, anthropologists, and psychologists have pointed out a host of theories as to why historic religious persons and communities have opted for belief. Philosophers have written about their own reasons and attempted to provide logical insights and argumentations for their faith, agnosticism, or disbelief. Some scholars have suggested that beliefs not only fulfill needs for communities and their members but also provide answers to all sorts of ultimate questions. Believing also changes the way people live because it gives them a type of hope or ability to live out a vision of the world. [1] While it has been known for a long time that religious belief can be a product of society, it has also become apparent that there was little separation in many societies regarding things are religious and things that are not.

People believe in all sorts of things under the guise of religion. Just because beliefs have been in place for centuries does not make them logical or true. One of the things that I really enjoy about studying religions of the world is that I get to learn about seemingly strange communities and their astonishing beliefs and practices. While few things completely surprise me, every so often, while reading about an "interesting" religious group or movement, the voice in my head shouts out: <u>really, do they actually believe that?</u> Even in the modern age, if nothing can be proven for certain, everything can potentially be believed.[2] Particularly in cultures where freedom of religion is practiced, there seems to be tolerance for all types of irrational activity and belief, whether it claims to come from the authority of a God, or just seems the culturally popular thing to adhere to. There are always reasons. Part of that freedom of religion is that we have to respect the rights of others to have those reasons as long as (it seems) they do not do a larger harm to persons or society outside the group. But what if they are doing harm to themselves (things outsiders can see but believers refuse to recognize)? The refusal of medical treatment among Christian Scientists is but one example. Yet we have not been able to save them in times of medical crisis, primarily because they have the freedom to believe in the power of God's (non-medical) healing intervention.

Studies show that the gap between belief in religious doctrines and religious membership in the United States has significantly increased. Some belong to churches because they feel the need for community. Others choose to believe but not attend community services. Scholars have begun to study and ask about the meaning of beliefs for modern adherents. For many, it is not about the beliefs, but the people who they gather and share with. When I was a young man I lived in Syracuse, New York for several years while running a youth program at a suburban Catholic parish. I was also the gym teacher for the parish elementary school. The old parish church building was so small that it could not accommodate the growing number of suburban parishioners who wanted to attend mass on the weekends. We would therefore transform the school gymnasium into a worship space each and every weekend, and systematically remove the makeshift altar and chairs before school began on Monday. My life was literally centered around the gym. One evening a week I ran a men's basketball group, just a group of middle-age parish guys getting together for pick-up games. Rather strangely, the very place where we gathered for sacred liturgy each week was also the place where we sweat and let off steam. At the time I was living downtown near the university in an apartment building with a bunch of graduate students. One evening, my neighbor across the hall, after seeing me in athletic attire, asked what I was up to. I told him about our evening basketball games and I invited him to attend. He played regularly for the next several months. Then, one Sunday, while I was on the altar giving a homily at mass, I spotted him in the congregation. I began to see him in more regular attendance after that. One evening at basketball, I decided to ask him why he chose to start coming to church. I never imagined that he was Catholic, and in an almost apologetic gesture, told him that I never had any intention of using basketball to lure him to the faith. He answered that over the months of interacting with the parish men at the gym he felt an increasing sense of connectedness to the community and one weekend morning decided to join the members and their families at that very same place for a different kind of fellowship. He remained a member of the parish community through his graduation despite the fact that our apartment building was completely on the other side of town. Community (not belief) can be one of the major reasons for people being religious.

So how can believers be justified in the faith that they hold? Clearly, being a person of faith is not just a matter of forming an opinion. While this seems to be a big question for scholars, adherents do not seem to be troubled by it. In America, still close to 90% of Americans (according to Pew and Gallup poles in 2016) still believe in some sort of higher power or God. Of course that number was much, much higher 30 and 50 years ago. Even for those who do not connect their life of faith to a faith community, belief is something more than just calling oneself a Lutheran, a Hindu, a Jew, or a Sikh. Certainly, a person can be a member of a religious community and not believe in a higher power. But belief constitutes something deeper that becomes part of one's life, even for those who say they are spiritual, but not religious. It does not have to be rational, it can be doctrinal (or not), and may even permeate to a level where we are not even aware, that is, to a place that is not always actively part of our immediate conscious thought. Jonathan Z. Smith has done work on the issue of whether people are being consciously religious (or not) in their approach to matters of faith. He suggests that scholars studying the religious experience should be willing to look almost anywhere to observe religious activity.[3] Smith also suggests that when in the engagement of academic activity, the true scholar should be paying more attention to the discipline of the process, rather than the merits of the actual beliefs themselves. That is, to the investigator, no belief or reality should be so sacrosanct in itself that one loses focus on the task at hand, which is impartially delineating information about practices and ideas. No faith is beyond scrutiny. Measuring and judging what is, or is not, sacred (or holy, or religious, or an article of faith) should be removed from the religion scholar's agenda. So is the discipline of religious studies then "religious"? Smith would say no, you do not have to be a believer to engage in religious studies. I tell my students this all the time when they first come into my class and they apologize for having no religious background or upbringing. It might actually be of some benefit to have no religious baggage because they are proceeding from a place of impartiality that other classmates do not share.

Belief is not always necessary to being part of a religious community, but it is necessary to truly being a person of faith. It is not personally necessary for a person engaged in the study religion. Scholars have used the term *homo religious* to describe the human propensity to be religious. It does not refer to one's particular beliefs, community, or religious institution, but an existential drive toward ultimate questions. Are we all *homo religious,* in some way oriented toward a religious disposition, or just potentially so? Is a propensity to believe wired into our brains and genes, or is it cultural? Neuroscientists have studied the brain using imaging techniques and have come to the conclusion that there are defined areas that activate when responding to religious stimuli. But these areas are also involved in non-religious activities like decision-making or abstract thinking. Most scholars believe it is an interaction of both the brain and culture that produces a human mind that is elastic, evolving, changing, and part of which has the ability to be religious. It is affected by the fact that we still live in a religiously influenced society and that within each individual has an active part of the brain that reacts to a surprising variety of religious stimuli that are products of our culture. While most of us have reactions of this sort (increase of activity in one part and a decrease in another), measurement of the brain activity is not exactly the same for everyone and depending upon the specific type of religious practice (meditation, chant, speaking in tongues) additional parts of the brain are activated, or are not. [4] The next question then that needs to be asked is: did God create this ability in our brains to communicate with him? Is this a product of evolution that causes order, comfort, morality, perceived religious alterations of reality, and hope in society? Definite answers to these questions are unfortunately limited to perceived realities, versus the empirically verifiable reality of a God.

Religion Returns to the Secular City

In 1984, Harvard professor Harvey Cox was compelled to revisit his famous Secular City scholarship due to the fact that there seemed to be decided shifts in demographics and increased interest in religious activity in America. Maybe God was dead, but TV evangelists like Jerry Falwell Sr. (1933-2007), Jim & Tammy Baker, Ernest Angley, Pat Robertson, Oral Roberts (1918-2009), and Jimmy Swaggart didn't think so, and they were making a renewed imprint on the American religious landscape. There were similar evangelists in South America, also those espousing Liberation Theology (which appealed to the economically and socially oppressed) who were making a dramatic impact. Church attendance was up all over, and even those who did not believe in churchgoing had found other ways to be religious. For some evangelicals, faith-healing was even part of the process. Outside America, religious movements in Africa, India, Turkey, Japan, and parts of the Middle East began to flourish. Even mainland China was beginning to allow some practice of religion to return. It was the height of the New Age Movement, origin of the American Buddhist movement, and *A Course in Miracles* continued its steady rise. Enrollment in Cox's classes at Harvard was at an all-time high. It is interesting to note that both evangelism (which in many instances was non-denominational) and liberation movements (which included the Black churches) were often anti-institutional when it came to established religion. Both movements claimed to be calling believers back to the earliest and original messages of Christianity, asserting that their ideology could be worked out in a modern context.[5] However, Cox claimed that the two movements could not be more different. The new evangelists played upon themes of nationalism, patriotism, individual blessings and success (many were comfortably watching these preachers on their own color TVs while sitting on the couch), and perceived connections between faith and the founding of our nation. The liberation movements were about social justice, supported the rights of the poor, were revolutionary in nature, antigovernment, and in favor of blessings for all (not just those who are saved by the special favor of a particular type of grace).

The secularization thesis of the 20th century had been influenced by the writings of Emile Durkheim, Karl Marx, Sigmund Freud, and Max Weber. These social scientists were writing in the early part of the century and depicted an evolutionary decline in the influence of religion upon individuals and institutions. This was due to modernism, the shifting views of the supernatural and changing attitude about the interpretation of revealed religions. Scholars came to accept the notion that secularization would erode religious sensibilities causing them to be replaced by reliance upon reason and the modern sciences (both social and physical).[7] Religious denominations themselves would falter. They predicted that religion would first lose its grip on institutions then eventually upon individuals. Modern individuals would become increasing less dependent upon God, religion, and religious experts or religious institutions for direction. We saw this trend crescendo in America during the late 1960's with the Secular

City and Death of God. The revival of religion and the decline of secularization in the 1980's caused a stir among academics. Religion scholar Ross Aden writes: "The secularization thesis had such a hold on the study of religion that the announcement of its demise was unsettling to the field of religious studies".[6] There was an increase in the visibility of religion not only in America but in global politics and religious movements worldwide. A new discussion about the place of religion in public life among religious scholars needed to take place.

As Scholars and Students of Religion, How Should We Approach Forms of Fundamentalism?

In the case of religion, for many fundamentalists, the historical/critical method is considered a contortion of reality. With the comeback of religion in America after the "death of god period" some of the greatest gains came in the fundamentalist churches and communities. I happen to teach in an area of the country where there is a growing number of Muslims. For many, the issue of fundamentalism is a difficult struggle. Others have embraced the fundamentalist stance as part of who they are. Given this current educational landscape fraught with pitfalls and major questions, a professor often has to tread with some care. I want my students to understand that the manner in which religious phenomena, experience, philosophy and scholarship are interpreted, depicted, and presented to subsequent observers, can be affected by the agenda of the chronicler (be it conscious or unconscious). Chroniclers could be modern, but are often ancient or medieval. As we have mentioned, many see a divine authorship in the scriptures. This is a major game-changer because then we then have to interpret God's agenda, or what the historically perceived agenda of the divine was at the time of the writing. Similar elements hold true methodologically for both the disciplines of History and of Religion. In fact, the early academic field of The Study of Religion was often referred to as The History of Religion. Now I think The Study of Religion deals with a few additional existential matters. The trick in Religion classes is to get students to accept that notion that religious "revelations" and spiritual inspiration can be studied historically and sociologically. In the discipline of History, while there can be consensus, students need to understand that each source is but one point of view. It gets more complicated when someone believes his or her point of view is the eternal truth. Prevailing opinion, tradition, logic, prejudice, or sources of authority are often not enough to stop those who are have already committed themselves to an idea or practice that can give new meaning and inspiration to their work, perspectives, lives, or viewpoints. Among the things I have chosen to examine in my doctoral and professional studies are how groups as well as individuals are able to work out their senses of perception, truth, goodness, value, and "ultimate reality". It has not been too difficult to carry this into the classroom. When it comes to the study of history it is important to have a sense of how (and if) we can truly know things of the past, how much of it is colored by our perceptions or the perceptions of those that have preceded us, and what any of it has to do with the direction our world and cultures are headed. In The Study of Religion, it is often a question of getting students to respect the beliefs of others and to respect the study of those beliefs (even when they believe them to be wrong).

Back when I was teaching at Ohio State I was responsible for supervising a number of graduate teaching assistants (TAs). My class of about 200 students was divided into 6 or so smaller sections, each supervised by a TA. The whole group would meet in a lecture format in a huge auditorium twice a week (where I taught) and the graduate TAs would meet separately with the groups they were assigned to once a week for discussion. The TAs would grade exams, manage the paperwork for each of their small sections and could also give their own assignments or lead small group exercises. As the instructor of record, one of the things that I disliked most about this system was the fact that I frequently had to intervene over complaints and squabbles between students and teaching assistants (many of the TAs were senior to their students by only a few years). One of the things the TAs would often do is allow students to give presentations in their small sections. I recall a particularly troublesome grade dispute between a student who was a fundamentalist Christian (fully believing in the inerrancy of the Bible) and her TA. The student had given a presentation on the point of view of her denomination or religious community and the TA gave her a zero (0%) on the assignment, telling her that fundamentalist viewpoints had no place in the study of religion. (I know of fundamentalist Christian colleges where the student would have received a zero if the presentation did not contain a literal biblical component.) Seeing as we were at a publicly funded institution and studying World Religions, the student complained that her faith group was being discriminated against. The TA had no tolerance for fundamentalism and would not back down. In fact, I found out later on that she had somewhat of a personal mission to stamp out the ideology. Her argument (I'm paraphrasing) went something like this: "What if we were in a biology class? Would a creationist point of view have been tolerated? Absolutely not. The Study of Religion is a science, just like all other disciplines and should be treated that way. I will not have fundamentalist views taught in my classroom. It is not the proper academic approach." I had to remind her that it was technically my class, that she was also a student, and I was still responsible for what went on. I tried to persuade her that every religion, even the ones you disagree with, must absolutely be treated in their own light. Students should not be discouraged from their personal beliefs or penalized because of them. I told her she could teach about and model the methodology of religious studies without infringing upon the rights of students to believe and express articles of their faith. The study of religion can't solely be about pointing out the scholarly errors of fundamentalism, it's about making sure each religious voice and story (that we have time to cover) are treated equally to all others. Both respect and suspicion are part of the methodology (not one or the other). I also mentioned she might have intervened in the "preaching" part of the presentation, reminding the class that this was a particular point of view that we need to learn about within the proper context of the history of Christianity.

For a long time I have had a "no preaching" rule in my classrooms. During formal presentations and in discussions, information could be presented on any group, or their perspective, but students cannot present as "fact" articles of faith. They must treat beliefs as faith statements (or points of view), and they can't try to convince their audience or classmates that their beliefs are absolute eternal truths. The problem is that there can be a fine line between teaching and preaching. Even persons trained in the profession of religious studies are regularly capable of crossing it. Early in my career I had a similar issue occur (as the one I previously described at OSU) in one of my own classes with a student who was giving a presentation on the Pentateuch (the first 5 books of the Bible). The student also happened to be a part-time instructor in the Communications Department (she taught public speaking) at our college. Although we had studied the historical-critical method of interpreting the scriptures, she chose to totally ignore that point of view. Her presentation was aimed at persuasively convincing the class the truths of a creationist perspective. (A tall task even for a speech professor.) Her audience (the class) did not buy it, and because she did not completely succeed in presenting a balanced body of information, I did not give her a top grade. During the question and answer period of the presentation, one of the atheist students in the class completely lit her up, and did a fine job of logically deconstructing the creationist position. While I intervened occasionally in the heat of the discussion, trying to buffer points of view, I basically let the pillory happen (figuring the instructor capable of handling herself). Embarrassed and angry that she did not get an "A", my student (the speech instructor) went to my chair and complained. The fallout was uncomfortable for all concerned and I learned a valuable lesson about keeping such discussions under control. While there is room for an emotional element, it is best to keep discussions limited to facts about beliefs, suspending all judgments about ultimate truth and how careful we need to be when dealing with, preserving, respecting, and presenting the issue of belief itself. What is so ironic about this story is that the atheist student did not finish the class. She dropped out sometime at the end of the semester but appeared again a number of years later in one of my classes, "born again". No longer an atheist, she had come to some appreciation of faith, a perspective that required some suspension of the existential logic that colored her previous viewpoints. Sometimes students ask me: why should we study atheism if it is not a religion? The simple answer is that atheism is a historical ideological movement or viewpoint, related to religion, which deals with some of the same problems of all religions in regard to the matters of belief. It just comes to different conclusions. Religion and human faith are curious things. Individuals, institutions, and doctrines evolve to meet personal needs, searches for illusive truths, and the needs of society. For some, as we have seen, the traditional God is not a need.

False Impressions of Other People's Religions

When I first started teaching World Religions at the college level I recall taking a group of students early one Saturday morning to the Hindu Temple in Powell, Ohio. We were warmly greeted by one of the priests of the temple and were treated to a first class tour of their worship space and the community facilities. At the end of his presentation he asked for questions and as is often the case, I was embarrassed to find my students stone silent. After what seemed to be an awkward eternity I thought I would get the ball rolling and continue with familiar themes from our class discussions, which recently included the topic of reincarnation. I asked: "Do you know who you were in a previous life?" To which the priest began to laugh and then pointed out that it was not important to know where he had been in a previous life, but to where he might be headed in the next. Certainly, a wise answer. Obviously, most other Hindus also did not know about their previous incarnations. While I found the exchange slightly embarrassing, it was particularly instructive for me on a number of levels. First it let me know that something I would have been personally and immensely intrigued by (who I might have been in a previous life) was of little importance to a Hindu religious leader. Because of my own keen interest in history, I assumed that would have been something important to me if I were a Hindu. It made absolutely no sense to me that adherents to the doctrine of reincarnation not be interested in who they were in former lives. Obviously, I was looking at Hinduism the wrong way (through my personal and Christian upbringing). Did I subconsciously want him to not know about a previous life because I did not believe reincarnation? Or, was I secretly hoping that he absolutely knew about his former lives, which would draw me more closely to accepting the spiritual beliefs of others. Another instructive point was the fact that the very person teaching about transmigration of souls did not know who he was in a previous life. This led me to see that Hindu religious leaders were as capable of seeing their doctrines interpreted metaphorically when struggling with the mysteries of their faith, as I (a former Catholic seminarian with 3 graduate degrees) was.

Women in the Study of Religion

While the practice of religion included a number of prominent women from the 1600's through the early 1900's, such as Theresa of Avilla, Jeanne Guyon, Ann Hutchinson, Jane Wardley, Ann Lee Stanley, Sarah Osborn, Katharine Drexel, Elizabeth Ann Seaton, Mother Cabrini, Catherine Booth, Mary Baker Eddy, Ellen G. White, Phoebe Palmer, Louisa Maria Hubbard, and Hannah Whitall Smith, the role of women in the academic study of religion, theology, and philosophy remained fairly minor. Most were visionaries who claimed to have received God's direct revelation. Many went on to serve as ministers and leaders for congregations, communities, denominations, missions, and various movements. Mary Riggs and Sue McBeth, Catherine Brown, Lucy Rider Meyer, Olympia Brown, Isabella Thoburn, Charlotte Diggs Moon, Antoinette Brown, and Aimee Semple McPherson were among them. Some were famous activists and champions of social justice like Elizabeth Fry, Helen Hunt

Jackson, Sarah and Angelina Grimke, Hariett Tubmann, Sojourner Truth, Sarah Winnemucca, Jane Adams, Frances Willard, Vida Dutton Scudder, Annie Besant, Lenora Barry, Mary Kenney O'Sullivan, and Dorothy Day. Women involved in the academic study of religion remained much in the background, literally until the late 1960's or early '70's. In fact, most of these pioneers are still alive today: Mary Daly (1928-2010), Annemarie Schimmel (1922-2003), Rosemary Radford Ruether, Elaine Pagels, Karen Armstrong, Wendy Doniger, Diana Eck, Linda Woodhead, and Asma Barlas,[8] to name a few.

One of the movements that probably did the most to advance the place of women in the academic study of religion was that which took up the plight of the 19th century feminist critique of religion. These voices not only criticized interpretations of traditional religion, but also ostracized churches for preventing women's advancement in ministry, leadership, and education. Frances Wright (1795-1852) was one of the earliest female critics of religion in America. A Scottish born radical socialist, Wright spent some time in America living in utopian communities and traveling about giving lectures and speeches. She wrote about how traditional religions (especially Christianity) were irrational and had impeded human progress in the post-enlightenment age. Wright indicated that the power of clerical leadership was particularly detrimental to women. Detractors called her "The Great Red Harlot of Infidelity". She noted that women had so many fewer opportunities for education compared to men and that women's status was narrowly relegated away from religious leadership where their natural abilities and inclinations would be most suited. She wrote:

> *I will ask if two professions do not now rule the land and its inhabitants? I will ask, whether your legislatures are not governed by lawyers and your households by priests? And I will farther ask, whether the deficient instruction of the mass of your population does not give to lawyers their political ascendancy; and whether the ignorance of women be not the cause that your domestic hearths are invaded by priests.*[10]

Margaret Fuller (1810-1850) took the next step as a feminist critic of religion. Schooled by her father in a rigorous course of classics and Latin language she joined the transcendentalist movement in her hometown of Cambridge, Massachusetts. Margaret became involved in informal introduction of young women to higher education and later edited the transcendentalist journal, the *Dial*. She was critical of certain literal aspects of the Bible and believed that the spirt of the divine extended to many movements outside of Christianity. Her work on women's rights, abolitionism and rights for Native Americans allowed others to stand on her shoulders.

While known for her political and social activism and pioneering work over women's rights, Elizabeth Cady Stanton (1815-1902) along with Matilda Joslyn Gage (1826-1898) saw the Christian church as one of the greatest obstacles to the advancement of women.[11] They believed as members of the Protestant tradition, women should be allowed interpretation of the scriptures guided by their own reason, not the church's authority. In 1881 Stanton organized a committee of over 20 women to write biblical commentary upon parts of scriptures that pertained mainly to women. Called the *Woman's Bible,* commentaries of the parts of the *Old Testament* were published in 1895, the remainder and *New Testament* in 1898. Stanton questioned the blame of Eve for the fall of humanity along with the concept of divine revelation as transmitted to a number of the writers of sacred scripture. She rejected the biblical notion of man's dominion over woman, the virgin birth of Jesus, and even was open to the notion of a God who contained both genders. [12] When Stanton prayed it was often to: "Heavenly Father and Mother". While the Women's Bible was received with much success there were many (including some women) who were openly disparaging of it. Gage's work, *Woman Church and State* (1893), was an even more radical condemnation of the Jewish and Christian scriptures, which were seen as tools for the degradation of women. Corrupt and selfish male dominion over Church and state was supported throughout the Bible as a model for by religious structures and governments. Both reformers encouraged women to reject literal biblical interpretations and suggested that because of its male oriented structure it might even be impossible to reform Christianity and its institutions from within.

It would not be until the last quarter of the 20th century that women scholars were able to revisit some of the biblical arguments of Stanton and Gage to support a more widely accepted feminist critique of religion. Support for women's ordination in the Protestant churches, along with more gender conscious historical critical reading of the scriptures saw the very questions raised by the 19th century feminist writers finally coming to light. Other modern religious interests influenced by these pioneers include a taking into account of sexist interpretations in world scriptural texts, critique of gender-bias practices in world religions, renewed discussion of feminine aspects of the divine, corresponding interest in the feminine elements of Gnosticism, and a rejuvenated discussion of the goddess in ancient religions (brought up by Gage) which influenced much of Neo-Pagan practice and belief.

1. John Whittaker, "D.Z. Phillips and Reasonable Belief", International Journal for Philosophy of Religion" 63, nos. 1-3 (2008), pp. 103-129

2. Ross Aden, *Religion Today: A Critical Thinking Approach to Religious Studies*, Rowman and Littlefield (2013).

3. Jonathan Z. Smith, *Relating Religion: Essays in the Study of Religion*, University of Chicago Press (2004).

4. "Inside the Religious Brain" Chapter 5 in Aden's *Religion Today: A Critical Thinking Approach to Religious Studies.*

5. Harvey Cox, *Religion in the Secular City: Toward a Post-Modern Theology* (1984), p.25.

6. Aden, op. cit., p. 299.

7. Rodney Stark, "Secularization R.I.P" in *The Secularization Debate*, Rowman and Littlefield (2000), p.44.

8. Asma Barlas is an Islamic scholar who works on a critique of the masculine influence in Quranic texts. She believes Muslims should be free to have their own interpretations of the sacred scriptures.

9. Frances Wright, *Life, Letters and Lectures* Arno Press, 1972, p. 25.

10. Susan Hill Lindley, *"You have Stept out of your Place": A History of Women and Religion in America*, Westminster John Knox Press (1996), p. 289.

11. Elizabeth Cady Stanton, *The Woman's Bible,* Pacific Publishing (2010).

Chapter 7

Methodology and Objectivity in The Study of Religion

Some Personal Thoughts

As much of my academic training has been in the area of religion, as well as the history of cultures that are ostensibly religious, I felt it might be important to delineate some of my own thoughts on these content areas that I have over the years endeavored to understand and pass on to my students. Insights into the nature of religion can be derived from the study of ideas and practices that spring from culture, nature, tradition, or superstition, and are affected by inspirations, personal experiences, relationships, communal activity, and revelations. Both individuals and institutions have organized such thoughts and experiences into various philosophies, rituals, laws, systems and plans for living meaningful lives. Some have adopted these ideologies to orient themselves in some significant fashion toward "ultimate reality" or possibly the idea of God. As time goes on societies and groups preserve, modify, codify, interpret, or reinterpret the significance of these ideas and experiences within the context of both cultural and religious communities. For the most part, religious philosophies are born from the tensions between religious professionals (leaders, practitioners, clerics and contemplatives), religious scholars, in some cases secular scholars, as well as the common people who espouse religious practice and belief. Historical concepts are based upon accounts that have been transmitted in both oral and written forms, then collected, organized, presented, interpreted, re-interpreted, assessed, re-assessed and assigned meaning in light of our own contemporary cultures. Studying religion historically is literally an inquiry into knowledge of the past, a body of information that is acquired by investigating narrative, primary sources, and physical (and archaeological) remains, then using them as a basis of analysis. In my opinion, as students approach both the study of religion and the study of history they should employ a variety of viewpoints in getting to the analysis. I often find it quite helpful to incorporate aspects of Sociology, Literature, Psychology, Art, Music, and Science into studies of religion in order to obtain a wider range of perception. Throughout my own education, and in the process of educating college students from a variety of disciplines, I have found that critical thinking, a sense of the past, along with an openness and tolerance for many voices and opinions is what needs to be the true basis for any sort of liberal education. I also believe this type of thinking is the key to approaching ideological questions which no single individual, group, or discipline have been able to perfectly answer. Neither History nor Religion speaks with one voice. Paying attention to those many voices is what gives us a rich appreciation within both of those disciplines. However, it is also the distinct methodology of doing work within each specific field of inquiry that allows for some level of mastery to take shape.

Writing About Religion

The question of objectivity in any study is a slippery one. When I was working on my Ph.D. (which was the study of a group of monks in Western New York State), some of the members of my doctoral committee suggested I begin my investigation with a methodological section on disclosure. A number of writers such as Donna Haraway, Marjorie DeVault, Peter Novick and Mikhail Bahkatin have been proponents of the notion that complete objectivity is a relatively impossible thing to achieve. Novick says understanding the objectivity question, much like the writing of intellectual history, is like "nailing jelly to the wall." It "is not a single idea but a sprawling collection of assumptions, attitudes and aspirations... the exact meaning of which will always be in dispute."[1] Since the 1960's historians have attempted to move past the notion of historical relativism (truth is relative to whomever is telling the story) to theories of dialectical contributions to knowledge (different sides getting together, trying to get it right), which approached the notion of "practical objectivity". Scholars in The Study of Religion have used elements of similar historical methods but movement toward a reactionary return to narrative began to regain some appeal. However, as we saw in the chapter on the difference between Theology and Religious Studies, theologians generally proceed from a different point of view. The advice I have taken away from all this theorization is to proceed in my investigations with some caution, carefully utilizing approaches, which in my judgment seem to fit the investigative circumstances. No religious history or religious study can be perfect.

Telling the Story

As we begin to look at the evolution of religious activities, the history of human responses to phenomena needs to be approached. Descriptions of behavior and records of events, ideas and beliefs are important to grasp (at least in as much as we are able). Finding and verifying data is one thing. Interpreting it is another. Theological and religious concepts like revelation, redemption, transmigrations of souls, the working of grace, are seen as "metahistorical constructs" which transcend the historian's objective view.[2] In the process of historical inquiry, particularly with a topic as spiritually laden as the story of religious communities, how can a strictly empirical understanding of events be reconciled with accounts that appeal to acts of God for interpretive or explanatory purposes? As a monastic historian in the new millennium, I have asked myself these very questions. How does one adequately broach the issue of God's presence in all this? Especially given the possibility that there may not be a God, and the monks only think there is one.

The Case of the Genesee Monks – Issues of History, Spirituality, Perspective, and Voice

I have mentioned previously that I have spent much of my career writing about and studying a particular monastic order called the Cistercians. Significant portions of my masters and doctoral work were devoted to both medieval and modern aspects of the order. The following segment will provide some insights into the way one might go about examining a particular religious group using critical methods of scholarship. The case will demonstrate examples from my own study of one secluded house in the Cistercian order, a religious community that call themselves the Abbey of the Genesee. Donna Haraway, in her works on methodology has tended to include some sort of confessional aspect linked to her interpretation. It often becomes clear that her writing is shaped by her interests and pleasures. Not only are readers made aware of why she has come to a certain place or position in her writing but also how that has come to be. As you may have noticed, I have attempted to unfold a similar series of stories within the pages of this book in order to give the readers a better sense of the direction of my voice.

The Cistercians were founded in France in the Middle Ages in the late 11th century in response to a laxity in traditional Benedictine monastic practices. The order grew exponentially but suffered decline with the Reformation, Henry VIII's dissolution of monastic properties in England the ravages of the French Revolution. They survived into modern times; in part due to the success of a radical branch of the order know as Trappists (from the house of LaTrappe in France). The community monks of The Abbey of the Genesee who I have now been studying for some 20 years are one of the most austere and conservative religious houses in the United States. My interest in the order began primarily out of curiosity and the fact that I have a friend and former roommate who belongs to that community. The fact that there are still monks around is quite important to me, particularly because I think there are elements of their lifestyle that are worth preserving. I am often forced at great length to defend contemporary monastic lifestyles in the Christianity classes that I teach at a predominantly Protestant college or in my Comparative Religion classes at a secular community college. While I do deeply respect the contemporary monastic spiritual nature and the struggles of "religious" to find meaning in their lives, I can't help but think that they are prisoners of narrow circumstance. While elements of the lifestyle might be very freeing, other elements serve to limit their human and intellectual potential. Most of the monks themselves do not see it that way, or they would have left the monastery a long time ago.

My account of the Genesee monks was somewhat a reflection of who I was in relationship to my observations. Coming from a background as a former seminarian that for a time also lived a somewhat structured religious life, I can relate in some small way to the framework of their existence. In a more modified sense, part of our day was to be set aside for work (house jobs) and private prayer. The biggest difference was that we were allowed to have personal goods (music devices, sports equipment, cars, etc.) and when we had free time we were allowed to come and go as we pleased. In my study, research, interviewing, and writing about this modern group of Cistercians, the work produced was framed by what can be construed as fact, some information was colored by theory, the responses of my sources to their perceptions, along with my own personal response to all of. Critical methodologist and sociologist Marjorie DeVault has suggested that writing is a form of thought that can shape the ideas of other researchers; it is an operation of social relationships, not simply a matter of telling what happened, but the fitting and filtering of a narrative into a format.[3] DeVault has also devoted considerable research to the issue of standpoint. As writing is not a "transparent medium" through which authors convey truths, there is a certain "construction" and "controlling of meaning" which takes place in the process of the craft of re-telling a story.[4]

In thinking of my approach to interpolating the communal, spiritual and theological essence of the Genesee community, it might be useful to use what Stephan Bevans calls the "Transcendental Model" for writing about their experiences. If they are a community who is constantly listening for God, I need to be listening to their listening with an open mind, or better yet, when visiting the monastery I might attempt to listen for God in a similar fashion. Because the transcendental model of contextual theology puts so much emphasis upon the authenticity of the subject as a person who is attempting to experience his or her faith, it seems clear that the best person to comment upon a theological tradition is a person in that particular context.[5] So as a writer attempts to appropriate an understanding of the ideas, beliefs, practices and stories of others, these ideas would of course first filter through the writer's own context, but what one might be challenged to do is to attempt a greater and broader authenticity by trying to more fully appreciate the community's context. How does the underlying sense of the contemplative in each of these monks allow for the community to be held together? If you ask monks about the most significant events in their lives they are not going to tell you about the building of a church or the cultivation of land. The important events are going to be spiritual events. It is obvious that their perceptions of events are all connected to God through the community and these experiences of God are the things that are most important, clear, and real to them.

Even in interviewing, while gathering oral historical material, information still needs to be interpreted from the context in which it is obtained. Ultimately, in the process of interviewing, the interviewer becomes part of the context.[6] In that fashion, the interviewer might bias or affect the response of source. Does less interaction yield a more genuine response? I did not find this to be the case in my own interviewing of sources. In fact, the more removed I was from the subject, the less willing the interviewees seemed to be in terms of opening-up. Empathy and continued gentle questioning seemed to yield the most spontaneous (and I believe genuine) results. However, in an interactive fashion, it is also quite possible that a dialogue between my own perspectives and biases occurred as a result of the interview. What the interviewees told me might possibly have been expressed in a slightly different way, depending upon another interviewer (insider, outsider, scholar, news reporter, etc.). How the interviewer was perceived and what the source thought might be done (type of publication, archive, etc.) with their information may also have an effect upon the accounts which are rendered.

What has draws me to this modern study is the same thing that drew me to a previous interest in medieval monks. It is a curious fact that the Genesee monks are engaged in practices that average people are neither capable of, nor willing to do. They also believe they are living their lives with a noble purpose. I think the purpose, while in some sense is directed toward their own salvation, is also rooted in selflessness. Something powerful draws individuals to monastic life. This is a fact. Their lived example of trying to connect to life's meaning can be inspirational for many who believe in the things their lifestyle stands for. A number of these principles are rooted in the teaching of Christ. Depending upon their orientation, others might choose to believe that the monastic lifestyle is not even in agreement with the basic tenants of Christianity. Here are just a few common arguments: prayers offered by others are not effective for me; they are being spiritually selfish by closing themselves off from society; the mystical union they find is not "reality". How effective is the presence of monks in the world? It is effective to those who are listening to their story, the story I have undertaken to spread. But the fallout from the "secular city" and "death of god" in the 60's has severely diminished the call to monastic life for those who would choose such a heroic path. I suppose the same can be said for any religious ideology that requires a certain amount of sacrifice. It is clear to me we all are attempting to investigate Ultimate Reality in some way. Some are lucky enough to be able to choose a journey that is the right fit.

The Divine and the Historical Contexts

David Lotz, in an article entitled "A Changing Historiography: From Church History to Religious History" wrote about religious historiography in the United States undergoing a major change in the mid-1960's. He went on to define the period between 1935 and 1965 as a period of "Church History", connected to theology and community. But the history was also written in relationship to divine revelation, pivotally linked to God's redemptive act through the person and work of Jesus.[7] In some of the oral accounts that I used (several of which were tape recorded interviews from the 1970's) the theological/historical perspective comes ringing through. Religious historiographer Eric Cochrane reflected upon this earlier "Church History" in a 1975 article he wrote for *The Catholic Historical Review*. He stated that much of religious history had been written with a dual purpose in mind, not only to inform and recall a tradition, but also to propagate through historical chronicling the point of view of our own particular faith experience, while justifying and glorifying its existence.[8]

Lotz saw a much different philosophy behind the historical church studies, which were being done between 1965 and 1985. He calls this "Religious History", an approach that was characterized by a secularization of the discipline. The pluralism of American society also caused historians to move away from the biases that came with writing from within a particular group, tradition or ideology. New social historians of religion have focused upon extra-institutional dimensions, roles of the laity (particularly women), and smaller representative groups within institutions.[9] (Some of this was mentioned in the previous chapter). Religious historians began to highlight stories of people generally left out of the earlier histories (or in this case, types of histories). The answer to an adequate historical methodology in writing about and researching religious communities needs to be found in a careful transmission of the account given by the source (documenting through quotation or footnote). At the same time, care needs to be taken as to attempt not to give oneself over to the bias of any particular faith-based operative. However, keeping in mind that this is probably not possible, disclosure (as we previously mentioned) might be the next best option. In the telling of the story one must also be careful to not exclude the God-language of the source, and by disclosing in the account an awareness of our own interpretation or the coloration of that reality (if in fact we are aware of it). Care must also be taken to attempt to use the language of the source. In other words, we have to be careful about re-telling the story. The sources must be allowed to speak from their own time. For example, sources from the early period of the Genesee Abbey's history (1950's) are given from the viewpoint of "Church History". Many of my current sources are still living in a way that is quite attached to the world of the past century. While we are writing account in the 21st century, we are often using sources from previous periods. Chronicling has to be as objective as possible, yet imbued with sensitivity to the faith experiences of all those who tell their stories.

In an article entitled "Ends and Means in Church History", Henry W. Bowden wrote:

Students of religious developments now acknowledge that interpretations should be based responsibly on the limited materials of research findings... They see that retaining supernatural factors in historical interpretation appeals to an agency not found in record. It may be that God has acted in history as reality, but students tied to history as record admit that they cannot recapture that aspect of the past. Historians have to work with the partial evidence of human testimony. Such records contain many references to God, but there is no such thing as God's direct voice or agency in the human documents that constitute historical material... Most contemporary church historians have stopped trying to locate God in reports about what transpired...[10]

Both Lotz and Boden seem to think that we must set aside the notion of the hand of God in any factual sense during the critical analysis of events. To do otherwise would impose undue influence on the interpretation of one's research. I tend to agree. But the tension which prevails is one where we are now tempted to treat some of the God-language of our sources as containing certain mythological or metaphorical underpinnings.[11] We cannot ignore the issue of God if we are writing a history of a group of people whose daily lives, identities, and language are structured around a belief in their relationship with God. While descriptions of that experience need to flow through our work, it is certainly not necessary for us to believe everything our sources believe. In fact, it may prove to be an advantage that we not write from the same standpoint of the believer (even if we share that belief). Because if we do so, the work becomes "apologetic" as in the "Church History" period.

Objectivity in the Study of Spiritual Communities – Views of Outsider vs. Insider

When I was writing the History of the Genesee monks I thought it would be most helpful to understand things from their perspective (at least in as much as I was able). A way to do this might be to completely immerse oneself in the community. In the 1990's a friend of mine was doing doctoral work on the religious practices of a native group in South America. For almost a year he was living in a remote village among a tribe and studying their way of life. As he neared the end of his research and began to write up his findings for his dissertation he stopped short and gave up the project. He decided to completely start over, and began researching an entirely different topic in another area of religious studies. When asked why he wasted all that time and effort so close to finishing his dissertation he explained that he felt that publishing the material would be a betrayal of the community he was writing about. After living with them for so long he felt as if he had become one of them. He was no longer writing from the viewpoint of an outsider. By publishing, he would be giving away secrets (rituals, rites of passage, prayers, spells, taboos, practices) that had remained protected by the religious leaders of the tribe. Some religious historians have suggested that it is important to remain objective when writing a history that concerns sacred topics. Is it possible to be too close? For me, it became apparent that it was essential to at least attempt to remain open to the spiritual issues associated with the community knowing quite well there was no danger in becoming too ingrained in their way of life (at that point I had a wife and two young children). However, there was a famous theologian named Henri Nouwen who wrote about the 7 months that he spent with that very community of Genesee monks (back in the mid 1970's) that I was researching. His work is entitled the *Genesee Diary: Report from a Trappist Monastery* (published in 1976). It was not a religious history but was written from the standpoint of a spiritual reflection. By the way, Nouwen was a Roman Catholic priest and professor of Pastoral Theology at Yale.

If religious communities can be seen to be cultures unto themselves, how can an outsider attempt to accurately interpret their theology? Moreover, how could one be suited to speak of the experience of God or ultimacy in the life of a spiritual community of which one is not a part? A number of contemporary theorists (feminist, black, liberation, national or ethnic) have suggested that authenticity in such a venture is not quite possible. Stephen Bevans, in his book *Contextual Theology,* suggests that it is possible to participate in a context other than one's own if one is willing to be in-tune with a culture by learning the language, literature, custom and appropriate anthropological or sociological history.[12] We have historically seen some of this in the accounts and studies by early modern missionaries. However, in particular contexts, an outsider may actually be able to point out things which participants in the religious group may have never been able to see or attended to. Bevans suggests that a non-participant in a context can provide a kind of "counterpoint" through their critique of the culture or circumstance.[13] Addressing what Bevans calls the "shadow side" (negative aspects) of the culture could be easier for outsiders than insiders. However, the danger for outsiders is that they are not always armed with the depth of information and insights that have formed the opinions of those within. (While outsiders might not be clouded by the same internal and personal biases as the community that they are attempting to understand, outsiders are certainly clouded by their own perspective). Another important factor is the question of disclosure. That is, if one is coming from a contrary or even slightly different theological position, honesty in disclosing that position is necessary to the discussion. Bevins says this has much to do with learning who you are and who you are not. If one is to understand and write about a culture, then an understanding of context must be approached with both humility and honesty. The writer must also grasp that while he is on the margins of the community he has chosen to study, he never quite becomes a direct contributor or participant. It is through a dialogue with that actual tradition who responds in a listening fashion, that an understanding of the tradition by the writer, as both a stranger and guest, that the beginnings of contextualization can occur.[14]

Final comments on Perspective, Disclosure, Voice and Spirituality

The last issue concerning the way sacred history will be communicated surrounds an idea that comes from the work of semiotician (one who studies meaning-making) Mikhail Bakhtin (1895-1975). Some of Bakhtin's early work was devoted to a clearer development of communication by employing an understanding of the interplay between philosophy and language.

Bakhtin pointed out that transmitting information is dialogic (related to dialogue) and that one's context becomes critical to an understanding of the meaning of any utterance.[15] A study of a religious community is a conversation between the writer or scholar and the reader. It is my interpretation or opinion of a community, based of course on scholarly methods, which try to have objectivity. But even if I listen to multiple voices and try to weigh out all the various shades of interpretations, in the end, my sense of their (the community's) sense will always be flawed. As objective as I desire to be about their story, as reflective of their community I try to become, my writing about their lives will be mine, because of my own internal speech and predilection. The fact that this entire book has been written from a Western, Christian, male perspective is a complete testament to that. Anything that claims to be less (or more) would simply be "fudging" according to Bakhtin.

In framing the nature of a discourse that attempts to be (but never truly can be) objective, the problem of addressing spiritual issues could end up being illusive. Over the past thirty years in my academic treatment of religion, I try to think I have had success as an instructor due to the fact that I have been able to remain relatively neutral when unfolding the world's religious traditions. That is, I have had the sense to be able to point out the many sides of spiritual and theological issues with a hermeneutic of both respect and suspicion, while never being compelled to take too strong a stance. (However, I realize that by doing this I was in fact taking a stance.) I certainly can write academically about spirituality. However, when it comes to actual notions about relationship with God, I can only repeat what I have heard and then react to it. I cannot help but feel it is likely that ideas of God, Christ, Ultimate reality will differ within religious groups as I found they differed from monk to monk at the Genesee Abbey. Certainly some of their ideas have been much different than mine. How shared is our experience of God? If our ideas did not differ, we might in some fashion begin to approach the stage of some sort of religious programming. (I am not entirely convinced that the history of some religious traditions did not desire that sort of outcome or uniformity of conviction.) Yet, there seems to be some fine lines between communal spirituality, spiritual tradition, discipline, and freethinking. What lies between these lines are yet more interdisciplinary elements that we have yet to fully explore.

So, where does that leave the Genesee monks? The average age of their dwindling community members is somewhere in their late 60's. One Cistercian house in Utah has just recently closed down and there are others soon on their way to extinction. Do I think the Genesee monks are wasting their time and energy by living a medieval-like secluded life of prayer and contemplation? Certainly not! Any issues I have in interpreting their lifestyle and the major events related to their spiritual history is mildly blurred by the fact that there are elements of the monastic life that I strongly agree with, other elements that I do not, and still others that I do not completely understand. Let me share one last example. One of the things that I continually encountered in speaking with the monks was not their desire to talk about their history, but their desire to talk about spiritual things (that is, their spiritual history). When a monk tells me with the utmost sincerity that he has seen a vision, that God has spoken to him, or he has witnessed a miracle, the only thing I can do is record that information. What do I think? My first response as a philosopher and theologian is to process it metaphorically. I think he "believes" he has had such an experience and certainly some sort of experience (at least in his mind) has occurred. Personally, I am not certain how (or if) God intervenes directly and miraculously in our lives. Why? In part this is due to the fact that I have yet to fully comprehend the dynamics behind such experiences. I think our impressions of reality and our perceived experiences are what allow us to relate to questions of ultimate reality and thus define that reality. It is my opinion that the monks are responding to their perceived experiences of ultimate reality in the confines of their interior spirit and physically cloistered monastic lives. While I may not agree with the literal explanations concerning their spiritual experiences (miracles, visions, apparitions), I certainly am not going to say they are not real or true. Clearly something has happened which has profoundly affected them. The same is true for all the religious groups and communities that we will study. In fact, as a scholar of religion, I feel I need to be in a continual conversation with the search for that which lies at the heart of the experience of what German theologian Rudolf Otto (1869-1937) called a *numinous* presence. That is, I feel a need to ground myself in a greater understanding of not just what happened to a religious group, or what "appears" to be spiritually "real" to those who experience it, but to continue search for those comparative elements that tie those experiences together for all of us.

One of the modern criticisms of the phenomenologists of religion like Otto, Eliade, de la Saussaye (1818-1874) and van der Leeuw, is that they argue against the ability of a scientific study of religion to fully comprehend and articulate the religious experience, particularly those from the outside.[16] Otto dismissed scholars like Freud (and myself) who have never had a direct mystical experience or encounter. Critics would call these early phenomenalists exclusionists since they reject elements of the secular scholarship of religion that limit themselves to reason, the analysis of the social sciences, empirically verifiable data, and historical-critical methods (all the tools of modern religion scholars). Yet when it comes right down to it, isn't the quest for the sacred, or ultimate reality, what 90 some percent of all religions claim to be about? Ultimately, a sense for what Otto once described as *mystery, awe, and* wonderfulness,[17] coupled with what seems to be a human propensity toward the *sacred,*[18] are the very things that have continued to capture the imagination of adherents and keeps drawing me like some noble or romantic quest to continue studying and writing about traditions like the Cistercians.

Teaching and Learning About Religion

Morality, death, community, relationship with an ultimate source, questions about creation, and the issue of hope are the big prevailing factors in the study of Religion. In the face of all that has come before, we seem to be constantly re-balancing our understanding of reality and human needs in a way that will provide us with the greatest insight while hopefully leading us to answers regarding the attainment of the greatest possible happiness and good. At the beginning of each quarter/semester I continue to frame (for both myself and my students) the following questions: How does one's sense of ultimate reality relate to tradition, knowledge, the needs of present generations, as well as any possible projections for the future? How can we responsibly re-tell stories (particularly those of religious and historical communities) in a way that does justice to those cultures that have come before us while making their ideas understandable to those who will later hear, read, and experience remnants of their histories and traditions? In what new ways will contemporary society, scholars, and religious practitioners interpret traditions, stories, historical perceptions, morality, spirit, and material evidence in shaping our worldviews and the cultures we will become? How can I somehow continue to set aside my own evolving perceptions (or bias) in a way that will allow for the fullest possible range of responsible opinions to shine forth? These are the questions that drive my scholarly investigation. I anticipate that similar questions will drive the inquiry of my students. Hopefully I will be able to effectively continue to pass on an appreciation of these questions and their related issues to the learners in my classrooms and web portals.

1. Peter Novick, That *Noble Dream: The Objectivity Question and the American Historical Professional* (New York: Cambridge University Press, 1988), pp. 1- 7.

2. Stephen Bevans, *Models of Contextual Theology* (Maryknoll, NY: Orbis Books, 2002), p. 19.

3. Marjorie DeVault, *Liberating Method* (Philadelphia: Temple U. Press, 1999), p. 157.

4. *Ibid.*, p. 55.

5. Bevans, *Models of Contextual Theology,* p.106.

6. James Hoopes, *Oral History* (University of North Carolina Press, 1979), p. 85.

7. David W. Lotz, "A Changing Historiography: From Church History to Religious History", *Altered Landscapes*, Edited by D. Lotz, D. Shriver & J.F. Wilson (Grand Rapids: W.B. Eerdmans, 1989), p. 313.

8. Eric Cochrane, "What is Catholic Historiography?" *The Catholic Historical Review* LXI, No. 2 (April, 1975

9. Patrick Carey, "Recent American Catholic Historiography", *New Directions in American Religious History*, edited by H. Stout & D.G. Hart New York: Oxford University Press, 1997), p. 446.

10. Bowden, "Ends and Means...", pp. 85-86.

11. Henry Warner Bowden, "Ends and Means in Church History", *Church History* LIV, (March, 1985), p.87. See also Langdon Gilkey's *Naming the Whirlwind: The Renewal of God Language* (Indianapolis: Bobbs –Merrill, 1969), pp. 274-5 and 419-423.

12. Bevans, p. 110.

13. Bevans, p. 111.

14. Lotz "A Changing Historiography...", p. 318.

15. Mikhail Bakhtin, "Discourse in Life and Discourse in Art", *Contemporary Literary Criticism: Literary and Cultural Studies* (New York: Longman, 1998), p. 470.

16. Hilary Rodrigues and John Harding, *Introduction to the Study of Religion*, Routledge (2009), p.79
17. Rudlof Otto, *The Idea of the Holy*, pp. 25-40.

18. Mircea Eliade, *The Sacred and the Profane* (New York: Harcourt, 1987), p. 64.